Tom Stoppard.

Fritz von Westenholz

CONRAD ARMSTRONG

John Gilmer

FRANK NEWBOLD

A.N. Wilson

ANNIE SELCKE

Stephen Drucker

Chris Sweeney

David Brown.

Georgie Wilson

Diana Jane Perry

Harry Nelson

Francesca Kingsland

James Other

Michael & Judy Haslam.

Rita Young

DAVID LAKE

Nicky Haslam's FOLLY DE GRANDEUR

Nicky Haslam's FOLLY DE GRANDEUR

Romance and Revival in an English Country House

Foreword by SUSAN CREWE, Editor of *House & Garden*
Photographs by SIMON UPTON

For Colette, from Nicky

First published in 2013 by

Jacqui Small LLP
An imprint of Aurum Press Ltd
7 Greenland Street
London NW1 0ND

ISBN: 978 1 906417 85 7

A catalogue record for this book is available from the British Library.

2015 2014 2013

10 9 8 7 6 5 4 3 2 1

Printed in China

Publisher Jacqui Small
Managing Editor Lydia Halliday
Project Editor Zia Mattocks
Art Direction and Design Paul Tilby
Production Peter Colley

CONTENTS

FOREWORD

BY SUSAN CREWE, Editor of *House & Garden*

In his memoir *Redeeming Features*, Nicky describes his house, the Hunting Lodge, as 'quite simply the prettiest small house in the world' – and so it is, and at the end of this lovely book Nicky reflects on his luck of living in this sublime folly. Indeed, he is fortunate, but it's also true that the house is lucky to have him. I don't think there is anyone else in the world who could occupy and love it so well. No one else would have had the knowledge and the confidence to leave so much as it was in recognition of the genius of John Fowler (who had bequeathed it to the National Trust), while furnishing, restoring and adding to it with such charm and brio.

Nicky leads an extraordinarily varied and vivid life, and there can hardly be a person of interest that he doesn't know. He is no stranger to private planes and palaces, but in his own home he is down-to-earth, practical and sure-footed about what makes rooms comfortable, welcoming and easy on the eye. He is known to be a world-class interior decorator, a social commentator, a party giver, a writer, a blogger and now a singer, but he is also amazingly well read, an excellent artist, a talented gardener, a fine cook, a generous host and an all-round life-enhancer. He also has a phenomenal memory. All these attributes are reflected in the rooms of the Hunting Lodge, the furnishings of which Nicky describes as a hodgepodge, but I would describe as unselfconsciously grand.

Few small houses could sustain a forensic examination such as this, but Simon Upton's beautiful photographs that illustrate the book and Nicky's ability to take you by the arm and point out everything that will inspire, charm and inform you about his home make one wish that the tour could be prolonged.

Susan Crewe

MY STYLE, MY HOME

It would be hopeless to pretend that my style, at home, is anything but a hodgepodge of the things I love. It's an amalgamation of bits and pieces: some things inherited; some discovered lurking in far-flung markets or signalling from the dusty corners of forgotten antique shops; some are prototypes for commissions I have worked on; others are the result of wild bids in salerooms, or painstakingly tracked down long before the Internet made them a mere click away; some lusted after and finally acquired; several rarely regretted impulse buys; a few, frankly, souvenirs; and, of course, many, many presents from friends.

OPPOSITE A pause from a bit of strenuous hoeing in the box allée that leads from the garden to the conservatory, with the hornbeam hedges sporting their first green mantle of early spring. Soon they will be rigorously clipped into the tailored shapes that form the essential structure of the garden's plan.

Thus my style, if that is the appropriate word, is to find the way to house all these disparate possessions; to meld them into a panorama pleasing to the eye of the beholder, for we all know that is where beauty lies. The trick, of course, was to make that panoply of my particular taste pleasing to all those who see it.

But this accumulation obviously didn't happen all at once. Looking now through fading photographs taken in the early years of living here, I am astonished at how bare the rooms look, and how meagre the things in them; yet at the time they seemed absolutely perfect and, to me at least, as utterly pleasing as they do today. Maybe that is the essence of style – making whatever one has, or can afford at the time, attractive at that very moment.

There was no furniture inside the house the first time I saw it, aside from monstrous regiments of dead bluebottles, mouse-chewed carpets and the odd carcass of a chimney-trapped bird. But in each of the tiny rooms – not one is more than 3.7m (12ft) wide – the walls were beautiful, either coated with gentle blue-grey tinted limewash or a perfect pink-brown (exactly, I would eventually twig, the colour of fabric Elastoplast), achieved reputedly by an age-old East-Anglian recipe of distemper mixed with bull's blood; and, in one room, perfect, simple, trompe l'oeil panelling on soft-grey plaster. An overscale floral French *papier peint*, peeling and scuffed, lined the minuscule staircase hall. For years to come, until I asked Mauny, the paper's original French manufacturer, to copy it, I would stick down its luggage-bashed wrinkled runs with Copydex.

A Baroque carved, white-painted wood mantel surrounded the fireplace in the little sitting room, and a plainer one in the faux-panelled hall. Shabby curtains, some edged in fading hand-painted borders, fell forlornly at dusty windows. *Le Grand Meaulnes* and Miss Havisham had nothing on this sleeping, timeless *Wunderkammer*. And, strange as it seems now, I knew then that I must retain an echo of this *délabré* atmosphere; it seemed an essential element of the building's magical being. It also seemed that the house was telling me, silently but insistently, exactly the path to follow as I, in my turn, came to live there. I firmly believe houses and specific rooms, even new ones, have a voice and a soul. They will wince if one treats them cavalierly.

I was lucky enough to have been born and brought up in a gem of a seventeenth-century country house, Great Hundridge Manor, set in the chalky Chiltern Hills in Buckinghamshire. Its near 400-year-old brick façade had the same sunset glow as the Hunting Lodge, save that at Hundridge many of the bricks had been tin-glazed, so in the evening the house shimmered silvery pink. The rooms had the correct and amenable proportions of its period's architectural taste – square, for the most part,

ABOVE A watercolour by John Hookham of Great Hundridge Manor in Buckinghamshire, where I was born. It must have been painted relatively soon after my father bought the house, as there is no sign of the wing towards the chapel, which was added by Clough Williams-Ellis. Otherwise, its unassuming beauty is exactly how I remember it.

some panelled – with a longer, stone-flagged central hall. These interiors dictated decoration of sophisticated style, and though my parents were easily up to achieving this, they fortunately had, in the form of my father's great friend Geoffrey Scott, a brilliant adviser. Scott was the early twentieth century's acknowledged arbiter of taste, and his book, *The Architecture of Humanism*, is considered by many to be the apogee of the subject. He oversaw the furnishing and decoration both in the old house and in the new wings added by Clough Williams-Ellis, the builder of Portmeirion in Snowdonia, Wales. Scott's lovely schemes, virtually unchanged, were my surroundings as I grew up.

Thus, the rooms that I'd known since childhood were restrained and harmonious – Geoffrey disdained anything gaudy or precious. (And while I am now not anti-gaudy in the appropriate place, I find very valuable possessions slightly embarrassing, for myself or others – I have none in this house, but 'museum-quality' furniture or pictures, even in other people's, faintly disturbs me.) But as I grew, learned and looked, I began, of course, to hate them. I yearned for the spiky new edginess of the Festival of Britain's pallid chic, for the chunky modernity of rooms seen in magazines my American half-sister sent from New York, for the thin Vogue Regency of fashion photography, for the surreal (not that I knew the word) décors of certain films, for one loudly papered wall. One shudders now.

A few years passed. My mother, by this time, had a London house in a classical Regent's Park terrace. From here I explored the delights of city civilization and the people who lived in it. They opened my eyes to myriad other styles, no-one more so

ABOVE This painting, and the one opposite, are of Geoffrey Scott's rooms in the mews behind my parents' house in Hanover Terrace, Regent's Park. His taste in furnishings directly influenced theirs and, I suppose, indirectly, my own.

than an enchanting man named Simon Fleet, who lived in a tiny early Victorian house resembling a toy fort, in Kensington. His interiors – there were but two, one up, one down – were a mélange of the odd, the colourful, the cluttered, the exotic, the kitsch, the charming, and all welcoming, as were his friends, who were mostly in the theatre or design. Overnight, it seemed, my own rooms, even at Eton College, took on a look of theatrical ephemerality, a style I still find irresistible, if now almost exclusively for party décors.

Then a thunderbolt rent the chintzes and fringes of Mayfair and Sloane Street. Aimed with opportune accuracy from the god-like visage of interior designer David Hicks, 'geometrics' hit the custom-staled decorating ground with a lightning flash. His rooms were spare: square chairs, white or beige, sat squarely beside double-cube sofas set rigid to walls, standing on wall-to-wall carpet with small square designs. Uplights cast their dramatic chiaroscuro over vast, unframed Francis Bacon canvases. Metals gleamed and a square of black patent leather shone. It was an eye-opener, all right, and I awoke from my Beatonish reveries with a jolt.

But better not to abandon the trusted past for the utterly new. Early visits to Paris made me aware that the great decorators like Jean-Michel Frank or Emilio Terry knew precisely that: their parchment walls towered above monumental palace-like furniture and ink-dark framed Spanish paintings, or great slashy abstracts by Lucio Fontana and Pierre Soulages. Alberto Giacometti's ghostly plaster paled into significance, lighting eighteenth-century bronzes. Again and again, the mix of modern and timeless: the taste – for it was more than mere style – I would hope, indeed try, to assimilate.

So my first, rented, London flats had approximations of these stylish rooms I'd seen. One, all sleek greige and black, even had a Soulages on the wall, but painted by me; and it was my first lesson on the road to realizing that if you want to live very simply, you need to be rich. Pared-down purity shows every blemish.

Thus things changed when I was at last able to find, and afford, a house. It was a minute cottage – though, with its double-fronted façade, it looked far grander than it really was – wedged in wasteland between Waterloo Station and Bankside. I have always secretly loved several small rooms; those in Whittlesey Street were no bigger than any at the Hunting Lodge, and each could have a different character. I experimented with crimson lacquer walls, or coffee-brown tenting, with lilliputian bedrooms in blue and white, or green and white. Each contained interesting, rather than run-of-the-mill, furniture and objects, my growing understanding of such things nurtured by my closest friends, antique dealer Christopher Gibbs, beginning his stellar rise to *éminence grise* in this field, and Min Hogg, whose eye and wit would, a few years later, found *The World of Interiors*. The trend to hodgepodge for my own houses had begun.

But eighteen months later I found myself in Manhattan. Nobody who did not live in New York in the early years of the 1960s can have any idea of the sheer bliss of that city at its apogee, before downtown and uptown became homogenized into one physically and mentally bland, finance-obsessed town-blur, when every ten blocks the atmosphere, the sound, the smell changed, and Italian gave way to German, Chinese to Polish, Irish to Russian. There were mansions on Park Avenue still lived in by scions

ABOVE I love Scott's slightly haphazard arrangements of furniture. It was in these rooms that he conducted his torrid love affair with the author, poet and gardener Vita Sackville-West. The round bronze lamp on the low table is now in the staircase hall in the Hunting Lodge.

ABOVE My father's bedroom at Hundridge, before his 'St Ursula' bed was installed. The walls, as were several others, are exquisitely painted panelling, here in 'grotto-esque' style. Considered among the finest in England, they were stripped back to bare pine by subsequent owners.

or scionesses. There was Sam Cooke playing at the Tropicana, the Rolling Stones being heckled on 14th Street, Salvador Dalí at the St Regis, the Windsors in the Waldorf. Waspish East-Side widows still spent spring at their *hôtels particuliers* in Paris, and Los Angeles was ruled by a handful of society stars and took an age to get to.

And, oh, the houses! Cole Porter's bitter-chocolate and brass-shelved library on Park Avenue; Brooke Astor's chintz-flowered and real-flower-filled Ferncliff at Rhinebeck; the fashion photographer Horst's long, white converted stables on Long Island, hung with his portraits of Chanel and Visconti, and his portrait by Christian Bérard. Diana Vreeland, my boss at *Vogue*, entertained the world in her exotic apartment, a hellfire-red Oriental toile on the walls, while Andy Warhol had simply covered his walls with acres of BacoFoil. Billy Baldwin, the decorator who had made many of these rooms, and who encouraged me enormously, smoked incessantly in his brown-gold modern bedsit with its many layers of lacquer.

But as well as these delightfully luxurious private places, there were astonishing rooms installed in museums, brought over and meticulously assembled, entire and furnished, from various European palaces. Such interiors from great English country houses were among the first I had seen, as back home most were still wartime-forlorn and rarely open to the public. Encouraged by Philip Johnson, then most-lauded of ultra-modern architects, I would study them up close and unhurriedly, trying to understand the science of perfect proportion, the discipline of decoration.

The digs I found myself soon after certainly didn't contain any architectural merit, and were located in then-unfashionable Gramercy Park. The double-height, all-white studio had a tall (uncurtainable) window and a whopping plain fireplace; a wood spiral staircase led to a soon-to-be red-lacquer bedroom.

I found oversized furniture cheaply in Third Avenue junk shops, fake zebra-skin material in theatrical suppliers, and asked artist friends to paint huge outrageous Pop Art – it was *the* new thing – canvases for the walls. When photographs of my incongruous mélange appeared in the *Herald Tribune*, I felt a first faint inkling that maybe decorating could be my métier.

In just over a decade in America, I lived in a series of diverse places, first heading uptown to East 77th Street, a wonderful floor-through of a brownstone (above Woody Allen) where I flagrantly imitated much of the style I had recently been exposed to, and was flattered at the approval of those I'd copied.

Later came a ranch in Arizona, a long, low nondescript affair, the interior of which, by listening to its voice, I somehow turned into a fair facsimile of the Spanish American adobe rooms so vividly described in Willa Cather's 1927 masterpiece, *Death Comes for the Archbishop*.

This was followed by 1920s Hollywood's idea of an Arts and Crafts cottage, below Sunset Boulevard and nudging the Pacific. Its living room was barely big enough to squeeze my Harley-Davidson chopper into, that being, to me then, the most covetable object on earth. Our home needed no further embellishment.

Looking out over that ocean, one realizes that perhaps this really is the end of youth's road. It was time for me to retreat, go back through the dazzling mirror of America. I had seen and assimilated the most beautiful houses and the most exquisite rooms, known the people whose taste had designed them and the people who lived in them with such memorable style. It was time I put this knowledge to use, to create, for others and myself, a lifestyle that reflected, refined and embellished the world around me.

The rooms you see in this book are a culmination of a lifetime's passion for all these things. And the house's soul doesn't seem to object to the hodgepodge.

Nicky Haslam

THE HOUSE

AND ITS HISTORY

FROM HUNTING LODGE TO HOUSE

After crossing the South Downs from Winchester, the old road to London makes a zigzag to become the High – and only – Street in the ancient Hampshire village of Odiham, which in the thirteenth century bordered the grounds of King Henry VII's palace.

Nothing remains of this. Henry had built it because his nearby Odiham Castle – a stern flint edifice from where, 50 years before, King John had ridden out to Runnymede to sign the Magna Carta – was already falling into disrepair, even though much of its glinting ghost-pale walls are still standing. However, the palace's extensive park is to this day faintly defined by tracks and lines of trees that lead towards the great oak forests that were the royal hunting grounds, which reached from here to Windsor.

The Plantagenet and Tudor dynasties seem to have had a particular affection for this wooded landscape: beyond these great oaks lay an even earlier palace frequented by an even earlier monarch, Henry I. Then it was called Ormersfelt, but over succeeding centuries the

OPPOSITE The Jacobean Revival façade of the Hunting Lodge is an enigma. Is its date 1720 or 1740? In the Victorian era it was painted white with scarlet trim round the windows, hence the soft chalky pink of the brick nowadays. This addition transformed the conventional Tudor hunting lodge, on King Henry VII's royal hunting ground, into a delightful Revivalist folly. The house is surrounded by its garden – part formal, part flower-filled – and set, jewel-like, in the emerald forest.

OPPOSITE The plant stands on the brick 'apron' echo the shape of the ogee windows. I like white flowers near the house – tulips in the spring and geraniums in the summer. The low, curiously arched white doorway leads straight from the terrace into the sitting room.

ABOVE 'Versailles' tubs hold box pyramids and umbrellas of Portugal laurel. The stone figures are mid-eighteenth century and represent Spring and Summer. Each has a real instrument: a clay pipe for him, a tiny sickle for her.

name morphed into, and has stayed, Dogmersfield. Its royal owners dotted the woods with little brick buildings, mere lodging for shade or shelter from the chase. And, it was in one of these lodges that Catherine of Aragon, so the legend goes – a legend given strong credence by the fact that there is a house nearby named after that Spanish princess – first set her dark eyes on her betrothed, Arthur, Prince of Wales, eldest son of King Henry VII. The practice of engaged royalty to meet in forests continued for many decades; even Marie Antoinette first met the future Louis XVI in the forest of Compiègne.

The marriage of Arthur and Catherine was short-lived. On his early death, she almost instantly gave her hand to his brother, by now Henry VIII. The royal playgrounds moved away to another nearby estate, Elvetham, whose owner, Lord Seymour, was to hold elaborate *fêtes champêtres* for the amusement of the next monarch, Elizabeth I.

Dogmersfield, too, had changed hands. Given by the Crown to the Bishop of Bath and Wells, then to the Earl of Southampton, by the early 1700s Dogmersfield had become the principal home of the Paulet St John family. They were succeeded by the immensely rich Mildmays, who, in the fashion of the times, land- and water-scaped their vast estate, removing an ill-placed village, creating a larger lake and erecting, in the centre of a Rococo garden, a pagoda-like belvedere; from its topmost balconies glimpses could be caught of a series of distant eye-catchers, all in different architectural styles, ringing the newly created park.

Of this baker's dozen of follies, only one remains: a simple Tudor building, destined to be adorned in the early years of the eighteenth century – between 1720 and 1740, it is thought – with a fantastical brick façade. Looking southwest at the top of a broad ride mown through a wild-flower meadow towards a sheet of water – itself a relic of medieval carp-breeding ponds – stands King Henry VII's Hunting Lodge, apparently as flat as a stage set against a backdrop of swaying treetops.

During the summer months, the exterior of the house is lusciously ramped over by clematis, vines and climbing roses.

It is certainly a uniquely pretty building. Nikolaus Pevsner illustrates the garden front of the house, built slapdab on to the Tudor building, in his seminal survey of *The Buildings of England*, writing tersely that it has a 'pretended Jacobean Façade'. This is certainly true, for the windows and blank-arched gables are ogee headed rather than the more usual Gothic pointed. Half shut your eyes, and the building looks older even than the Dutch it is most obviously akin to, almost Turkish, and with a real stretch of the imagination, a hint of the Oriental can be detected. I often wonder, did the house's architectural style originate in the Far East?

Whatever its origin, the Hunting Lodge, as we see it now, is a bit of an enigma. Could its 'pretended' style, in fact, be a hangover from the preferred taste of centuries long past? Or is it one of the earliest, conscious revivals of Jacobean decorative architecture, a period that was not to become fashionable again for 100 years?

We will probably never know. What we can be sure of, however, is that the opening of the Basingstoke Canal, one of the earliest in the country, was cut through Dogmersfield's Park in 1795, and the southern area across the canal gradually fell into disrepair. The Hunting Lodge and nearby carp ponds, at their edge a tiny cottage known as Wilks Water, became silted, overgrown and uncultivated, and the house itself unmodernized in any way. In this decrepit state, it was lived in by some Victorian groundsmen or woodchoppers, one of whom had the unlikely idea of whitewashing the whole building,

OPPOSITE I always felt this side wall looked too blank and uninviting, so I made a false door. Later I discovered that there had been a door in this position before the original house was enlarged. The brick path that leads from the front door to the terrace is studded with setts of pebbles.

ABOVE LEFT The view to the lake from the old hall window. The umbrella-shaped Portugal laurel trees echo those in the tubs on the terrace.

ABOVE RIGHT Sheltered by the hornbeam hedge that encloses hidden gardens, Winter, with his real stick, gazes towards the distant water.

OPPOSITE Summer on her rusticated plinth on the edge of the terrace. Her sickle was away being mended at the time of the photograph.

Against a lush green backdrop of tall oak and elm trees, the fairy-tale façade of this most romantic building seems like a stage set. In fanciful moments I often think that the various statues dotted about the garden are like actors waiting in the wings for their chance to come alive and put on a show.

with geranium-red trim around the windows and doors. This seemingly eccentric idea was, in fact, beneficial to the charm of the place, as over the years the white was washed away, leaving traces on the grouting and pitted into the bricks themselves, giving the façade its mellow pink tone, a colour once described as fading rose petals.

So, this gem of a building slumbered into the twentieth century. Its owner by now was a Mrs Fox-Pitt, who, when not nursing her flocks of chickens and the gin bottle, half-heartedly began to cultivate the wasteland around it.

And it was in this state when, just after the Second World War, John Fowler – who, originally in partnership with the interwar hostess Lady Colefax and then Nancy Lancaster, a Southerner with dashing taste, created the legendary decorating firm Colefax and Fowler – saw the fairy-tale façade and fell in love.

History does repeat itself. And so it was that, some 30 years later, I turned the last bend in the rough lane through these woods, came to a clearing by a lake and, turning, saw this rose-pink, brick-gabled folly glinting in the evening sun.

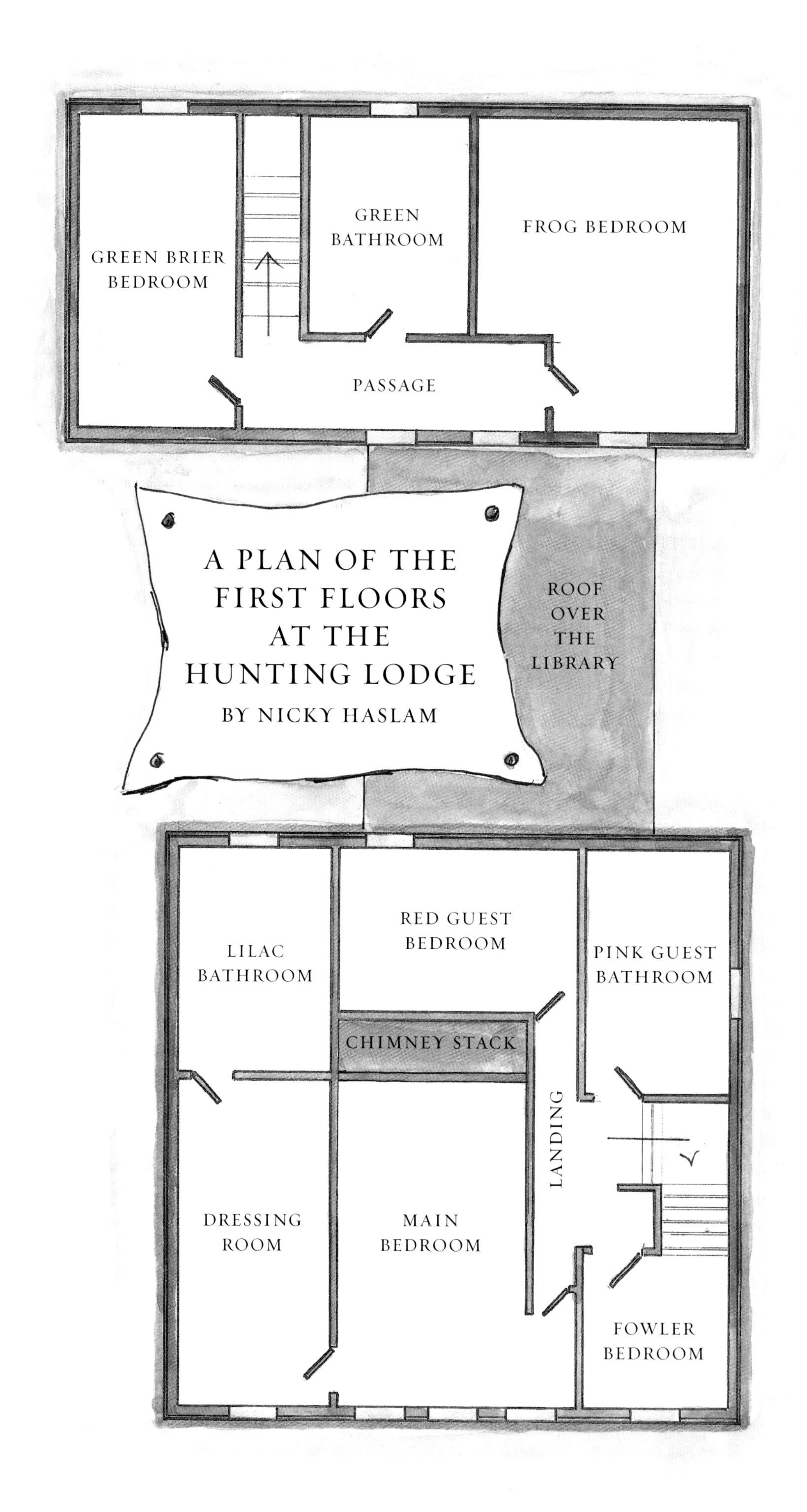
GREEN BRIER BEDROOM
GREEN BATHROOM
FROG BEDROOM
PASSAGE
A PLAN OF THE FIRST FLOORS AT THE HUNTING LODGE
BY NICKY HASLAM
ROOF OVER THE LIBRARY
LILAC BATHROOM
RED GUEST BEDROOM
PINK GUEST BATHROOM
CHIMNEY STACK
LANDING
DRESSING ROOM
MAIN BEDROOM
FOWLER BEDROOM

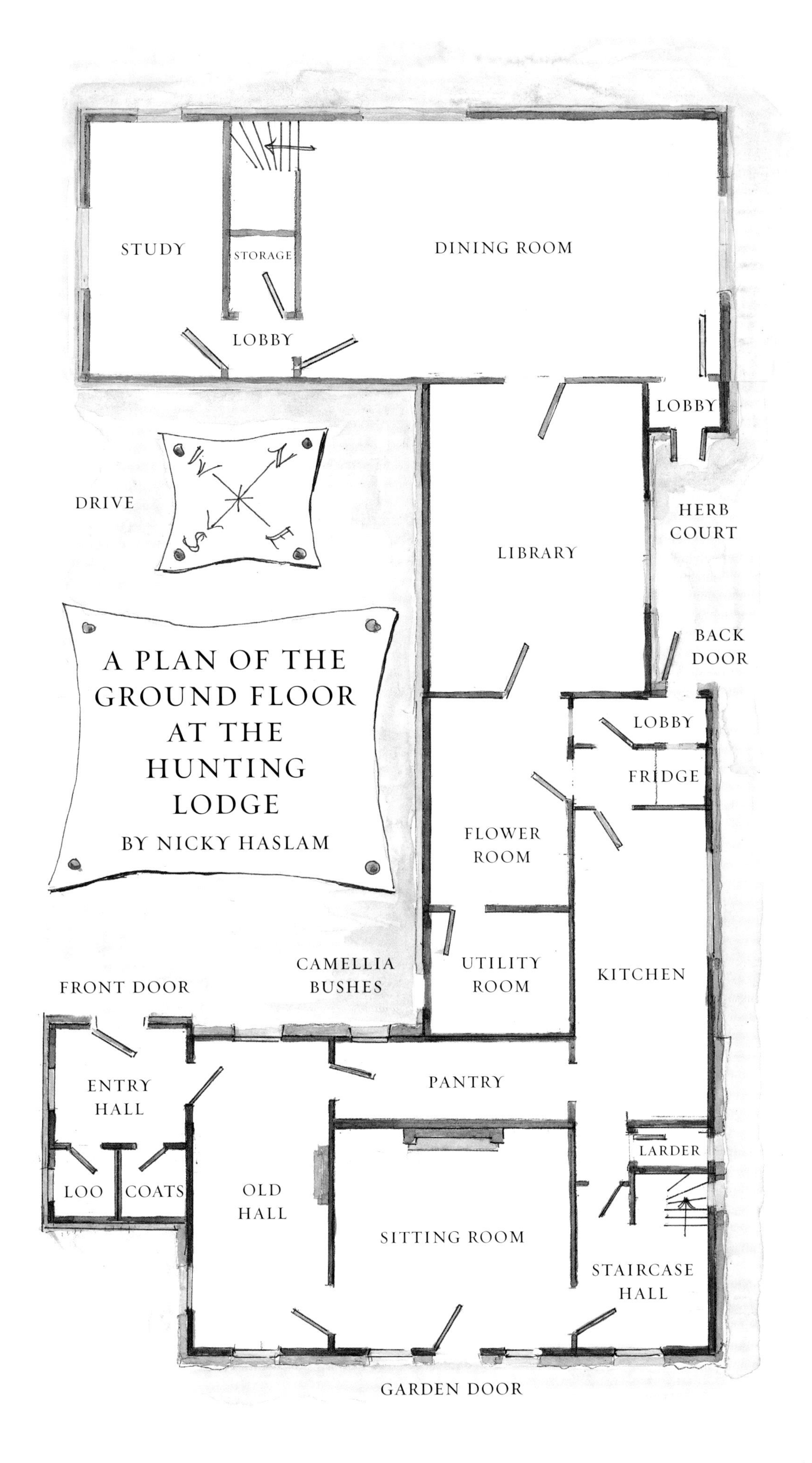
STUDY
STORAGE
DINING ROOM
LOBBY
LOBBY
DRIVE
HERB
COURT
LIBRARY
A PLAN OF THE
GROUND FLOOR
AT THE
HUNTING
LODGE
BY NICKY HASLAM
BACK
DOOR
LOBBY
FRIDGE
FLOWER
ROOM
CAMELLIA
BUSHES
UTILITY
ROOM
KITCHEN
FRONT DOOR
ENTRY
HALL
PANTRY
LARDER
LOO
COATS
OLD
HALL
SITTING ROOM
STAIRCASE
HALL
GARDEN DOOR

LIVING WITH
HISTORY

The customary conception of 'living with history', in the sense of inhabiting a historic house with awe-inspiring antiquity and a hushed reverence for a chronicled past, somehow doesn't apply to the Hunting Lodge. Its very essence, its light-hearted aura and its smiling façade manage to lift it out of fusty centuries past into a bright present.

That present is imbued with the romantic anecdotes of its gradual development from a humble hut to a comfortable home, still with memories, and the many legends – if legends they are – of those who have walked, danced, lived and loved in these tranquil atmospheric surroundings. Images – from Catherine of Aragon's sight of her first prince under dense boughs of oak, the courtiers hidden to watch her initial reactions, the splash on the lake of perch and pike landed by anglers for Dogmersfield Palace's noble feasts, to the clang, a mere furlong away, of labourers digging the course of the earliest canal in the land – hang in the deep, green shadows. Visions of rustics tending raggedy chickens and throwing handfuls of acorns to swine, and coaches bumping along the rutted highway between Winchester and Windsor lie on shafts of sunlight, while in iron-hard winter snowfalls,

OPPOSITE The mown ride up from the lake to the open garden gate is now flanked with wild orchids. This photograph was taken before I got to grips with the bracken. Like this, it does have a kind of massy presence, but I'd rather have the orchids.

ABOVE LEFT The diamond panes of the windows are set in lead. There is an incised signature of the glazier in one pane, dated 1871.

ABOVE RIGHT The latches are the original castings and are on every window.

OPPOSITE The old hall was originally the eating area. Its terracotta floor is buffed with Cobra Wax Polish from South Africa. A yellow linen cloth skirts a table piled with art books. The French eighteenth-century armchair is carved with musical instruments, its seat wide enough to accommodate the full skirts of a lady attending a concert.

one can imagine ice-skaters waltzing in time to the music of a tinny violin, as ragamuffins fling snowballs, and the steamy breath of shackled shire horses rises in plumes in the frosty air.

This is the history of this place, not dusty tapestries or worm-filled wood, no gory ghosts or headless riders, but sylvan simplicity. So much so that film director Tony Richardson chose it as the quintessentially English setting for Vanessa Redgrave's country house in *The Charge of the Light Brigade* (1968), while her father Michael paced the lawn learning lines for his last plays, and John Fowler, doyen of decorators, hauled the Hunting Lodge from Victorian vicissitudes to its timeless gracefulness.

Strong elements, architectural and ornamental, give a room structural form on which to base decorative flourishes.

When John Fowler discovered and bought the Hunting Lodge, not long after the end of the Second World War, the former gem of capricious architecture had become a mere poultry house. Over the next three decades he sensitively revived its eighteenth-century magic, cleared the scrub and laid out the formal, Dutch-inspired garden, which so perfectly and skilfully enhances the house.

I was fortunate enough to take a lease from the National Trust, to whom Fowler had wisely left the house, in the mid-1970s. While some wall decoration and brilliantly devised curtaining remained in the rooms, there was no stick of furniture. It has been my great joy, for nigh on 40 years, to furnish and decorate this romantic home. The results, shown on the following pages, will, I hope, delight the reader as much as they do me. So let's go further, let's explore the rooms, listen to the murmurs that the walls echo, and see what lies beyond. For behind this fanciful façade and the three rooms of the original Tudor building (now the old hall, the sitting room and the staircase hall) lie several more to be explored, rooms added piecemeal over the centuries, but in such a way as to create an intimate and harmonious entity surrounded by its equally enchanting garden and the forest beyond.

OPPOSITE The Baroque carved wood fire surround in the sitting room was installed by John Fowler. Its grandeur gives the otherwise simply painted walls a startling counterpoint.

FAR LEFT AND LEFT Early cast-bronze door handles and finger plates gleam subtly in the subdued light.

BELOW A Regency-style painted wood pelmet, carved in the shape of upturned shells, is positioned below the simple dentil frieze of the cornice in the entrance hall, which was added to the house in the 1950s.

THE ECLECTIC ESSENCE OF NICKY'S STYLE

WALLS

I fear it might be over-egging the pudding to extend my theory that rooms have souls by saying walls have ears, but as they have such a pronounced physical presence, maybe there's something to be said for treating them with respect.

Being an advocate of smallish rooms, rather than echoing spaces (except when appropriate), I tend to hesitate before wholesale 'knocking through' – and I'm not talking about plasterboard divisions – as there must have been reasons why the wall was there (to do with air circulation, heat gain or loss?), and it knows them. That first jab of the jackhammer always makes me wince, just as I do whenever I try to hang a picture, only to be left with bent nails, cracked plaster and a pile of dust. A wall will hear you discussing its future and dig in its stubborn toes.

While I don't go along with Edith Wharton's stricture that walls can be merely three colours, white, brown or red, it's not a bad concept to keep in mind. These colours, and their variations to greys, pinks and all shades of beige, work anywhere and are the most flattering to the human complexion, an important point, often forgotten. Blue and green, I find, are better reserved for light-hearted rooms for ephemeral occasions, though pale blue and green give bedrooms the freshness of spring. The hardest colour to use is yellow. Contrary to popular myth, it doesn't make a room feel sunny, and on a dull day it soaks up the sullen hues outside.

OPPOSITE A Sicilian mirror picture hangs on an elaborate silvered and hand-painted eighteenth-century wall covering in the little vestibule leading to the garden room. Above it is an early Colefax and Fowler wall lantern.

OPPOSITE In the new entrance hall, MDF panels surround the subtly painted door frames. The panels were simply applied directly to the wall and the whole room was then painted a scumbled stone colour.

ABOVE LEFT A portrait of Madame, the second wife of Louis XIV's gay brother, hangs above the book table in the old hall next door. She wrote the most deliciously bitchy diaries.

ABOVE RIGHT The walls in the old hall were frescoed long ago by George Oakes. They are the simplest form of trompe l'oeil panelling on a warm grey-brown background, with the shadowed and highlighted edges of the panels worked out with regard to the light source from the windows.

LA CIVETTA
LE CHIAVI

OPPOSITE In my bedroom the blue-grey dragged walls have strips of floral Mauny wallpaper border pasted vertically at regular intervals. This is a quick, inexpensive trick, giving height and colour to plain walls. The two larger engravings, in their original gilt-edged ivory frames, are Italian, depicting children playing games, a subject I have sort of unwittingly started to collect.

THIS PAGE Sweetly scented summer blooms mimic the colours of the tumbling flowers on the paper columns. In the dressing room next door, the wall plaster, painted in the same blue-grey, recently 'crazed' noticeably. Filling in the cracks left white patches, so rather than redo the whole room, I had the patches integrated as streaks of white marble (see page 163).

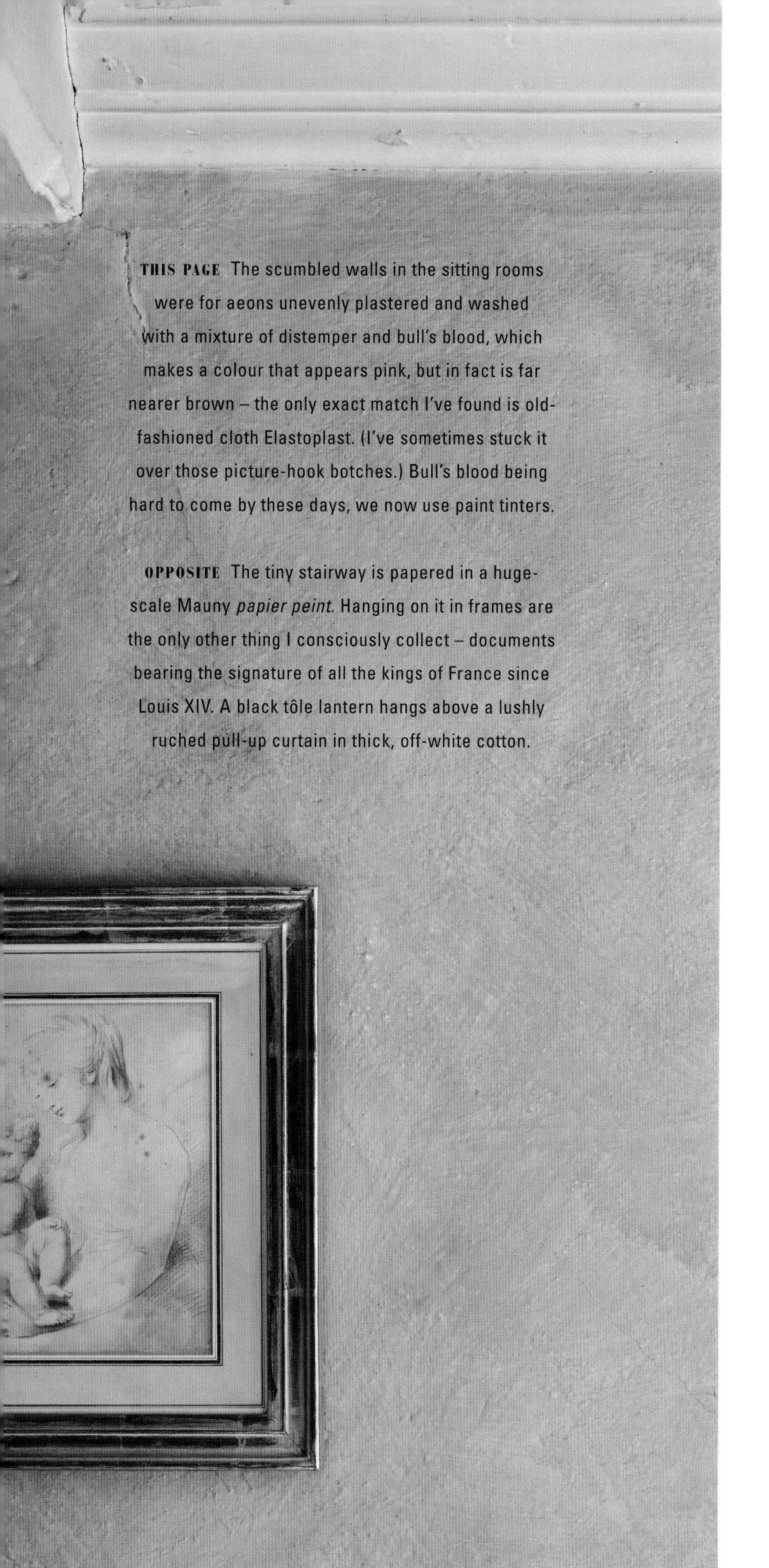

THIS PAGE The scumbled walls in the sitting rooms were for aeons unevenly plastered and washed with a mixture of distemper and bull's blood, which makes a colour that appears pink, but in fact is far nearer brown – the only exact match I've found is old-fashioned cloth Elastoplast. (I've sometimes stuck it over those picture-hook botches.) Bull's blood being hard to come by these days, we now use paint tinters.

OPPOSITE The tiny stairway is papered in a huge-scale Mauny *papier peint.* Hanging on it in frames are the only other thing I consciously collect – documents bearing the signature of all the kings of France since Louis XIV. A black tôle lantern hangs above a lushly ruched pull-up curtain in thick, off-white cotton.

So here in the Hunting Lodge this principle is maintained. Even the dragged blue-grey paint of my bedroom and dressing room can hardly be called full-bodied blue. The new entrance hall and old hall are both soft shades of stone and warm grey-brown, while the sitting room is a complexion-flattering pinkish brown. In the library, originally stables for a couple of what must have been very small horses, every surface, including bookcases and ceiling, is a deep, dark, pinkish red, which is great at night; as the room gets very little light, there's no point in trying to brighten it up.

Wallpaper plays an important role in the house. The staircase hall, when I came, had a huge old floral *papier peint* by Mauny, which taught me that using big patterns in small areas is a brilliant wheeze. Having since had the paper copied, by Mauny, I've used it several times in various custom colourways for commissions.

I recently redecorated a bedroom – so small that it can only hold a double bed, a pair of nightstands, a chest of drawers and a chair – with another Mauny paper of different-width red stripes on a white ground. I then used red-and-white striped heavy cotton for the bed canopy and blind, and plain red for the curtains. The bed linen is also red and white. Far from being dazzling, it is a surprisingly restful room.

One of the other guest bedrooms is decorated with a wallpaper I designed. Its pattern, stylized branches of berries in brown and apple-green, is taken from a nineteenth-century Spode china plate I found in South Carolina; its pure white background brings a summery radiance into the north-facing room.

beasts, bugs and botanicals

The only extravagantly decorated room in the house is the one I use for dining, but it is so pretty, it is nice to just stand and look at it. The walls, apparently covered in wide lengths of a vaguely Anglo-Chinese eighteenth-century paper, curling in places, have in fact been painted by Paul Czainski in imitation of a wall covering I was given by a client of John Fowler's. I get huge pleasure in that progression coming full circle.

Above this room, which was originally a separate building called Elm Cottage, is a whimsical guest room. Trompe l'oeil trelliswork covers the walls, and here and there in the diamonds little frogs prepare to leap to a new perch, while dragonflies hover on the wing. I am not a great lover of murals per se, but these little creatures amuse not only children but anyone who sleeps there.

OPPOSITE The painted 'wallpaper' in the dining room depicts strange exotic fruit and black bugs and birds, but the room is wonderfully ephemeral and light-hearted.

ABOVE LEFT Simple faux trelliswork and the occasional frog enliven the walls of one of the guest rooms.

ABOVE RIGHT I asked for this fruit-bearing straw bonnet to be incorporated, as I had seen one like it in St James's Palace. The crimson tassel provides the essential *touche de rouge* that every room should have; it makes all the other colours sing.

SOFT FURNISHINGS

The materials used throughout the Hunting Lodge are a mélange and no mistake. I tend to just bung anything together that I like, disregarding the dreaded 'co-ordination' theory, while keeping a vague colour palette in mind.

Textures, colours and patterns can all be mixed successfully through upholstery, curtains, bed drapery, tablecloths and cushions, as long as there is a unifying element to tie them together. Sometimes, rarely, finding the absolutely right thing, such as the plain pink-brown glazed chintz of the sitting room curtains, took longer, or maybe it was under my nose all the time and I simply didn't twig. Lots of the fabrics are favourites that I have used over and over again; some are now-unobtainable beauties – the printed French floral linens in the red library and the sitting room, for example – and some were generous gifts from friends. Sweetly, Lady Homayoun Renwick gave me yards of Colefax and Fowler's sublime 'Oak Leaf' fabric – now discontinued – when she heard I needed some extra material for a still-bare window in the old hall.

OPPOSITE I found this deep William IV armchair, with its claw and ball feet, in a junk shop in Gloucestershire. The Victorian Chinoiserie stool echoes the squares of the check covering on the chair, the colours of the chintz and check blending beautifully and toning with the deep red walls of the library. The metal coronet must have been a finial to some ducal gate: I had it made into a lamp.

VISCONTI

ABOVE In the garden room a riot of different floral chintzes cover cushions and upholster a pair of sofas in the vaguely Knoll style, which face each other on either side of the fireplace. I love mixing fabrics in this way. Classic rose-patterned chintzes, as fine as a Redouté painting, their naturalistic colours outlined with palest grey-mauve shadows, seem to me to be ideal for country rooms, and especially one like the garden room.

ABOVE In the garden room, a French canework fauteuil, with a cushion covered in the same wonderful chintz as the adjacent sofa, stands on an antique Savonnerie carpet, which has become delightfully faded and worn through years of use – all part of its charm. The roses and soft pinks and greens are the unifying elements.

OPPOSITE Another canework armchair in the garden room has a squab covered in 'Ric-Rac' material and a cushion in 'Zephyr', both from my new collection. The 'Ric-Rac' fabric, with its graduating colours, from green to black to red, was originally produced as a sample to show the three different colourways, but I liked it so much that it became the final design.

OVERLEAF, LEFT In the sitting room thick wool tassels in toning colours border cushions made from an old French flower-and-ribbon printed linen in pink and muddy green. The sofa on which they sit, and its twin that faces it, are slipcovered in 'Jaisalmer' by John Stefanidis, a hard-wearing off-white cotton. The covers are the same ones I had when I first moved here and they still don't need to be replaced.

OVERLEAF, RIGHT Warner's 'Fancy Lining', an oft-used standby, skirts a slipper chair. The French floral linen cushion has a deep fringe of dark, thick wool mingled with metal. Using unexpected materials, textures or colours for trims is an easy way to add a touch of drama and interest.

CAPTAIN JOHN SMITH
A LIFE OF PICASSO
A Chequered Past

I don't believe in the accepted view that all materials have to 'match'. I prefer to jumble up several different patterns, like a kaleidoscope. The eye soon sorts out the various motifs, and the vivacity is replaced by calm.

LEFT Another slipper chair in the sitting room, this time covered in Colefax and Fowler's 'Fuchsia' chintz. The cushion embroidered with a sleepy spaniel belonged to my mother's family, the Ponsonbys.

OPPOSITE Side tables, conveniently placed within easy reach of both the sofas and chairs, have been skirted with the same French floral linen as the cushions to unite the room.

Some fabrics in the house are actually antique, delightfully faded and aged – the French chintz used for my bed drapes, for instance, is more than 100 years old. Of course, a lot of the materials are, or were once, brand-new favourites, such as Colefax and Fowler's 'Fuchsia' printed chintz and Warner's 'Fancy Lining' (both seen opposite); I used 'Fancy Lining' in different colourways in both the sitting room, to cover a chair, and my bedroom, for the curtains. Several of the splashy rose or carnation patterns have had to be reinstated over the years, but John Stefanidis's sturdy white 'Jaisalmer' fabric, used to upholster my sitting room sofas, has stood the test of time, unreplaced for nearly 40 years. And, of course, I guinea-pig my own collections as they come out.

LEFT A collection of cushions made from early tapestry fragments and crewelwork adorn a fur throw on the leather sofa standing opposite the fireplace in the old hall.

ABOVE With its colours akin to the wallpaper behind it, the sketchy flower design of the seat cover on this naïve Gustavian chair, in the red guest bedroom, looks as if the stripes have somehow liquified when placed horizontally, making it charmingly unpretentious

Cushions, tablecloths, curtains and tiebacks often get deliberately 'wrong', or oversize or contrasting, trims and tassels. This instantly gives a jolt of unexpected character, there being nothing so yawn-making as a cliché.

So, on the whole, there is no actual fussiness in the rooms, but simply cut vertical and horizontal planes of colour or pattern, integrating, leading the eye smoothly ever onwards, with the odd sharp punctuation mark of surprise or wit.

OPPOSITE For years I couldn't find the right stuff for the sitting room curtains. Finally, I came across a plain glazed cotton almost exactly the colour of the walls. The door to the terrace, however, is dressed with ludicrously luscious, thick cream satin, held back by pink twisted wool ropes. I think it's called 'double duchesse', such as Victorian ball gowns were made of, and gives the door an importance.

RIGHT In the old hall, an essential log basket stands below the window giving onto a thicket of camellia bushes. The yellow pulling curtains are the same stuff I used for a tablecloth in the same room. The dress curtains and matching pelmet are in the 'Oak Leaf' fabric by Colefax and Fowler that was given to me by Lady Homayoun Renwick.

BELOW Off-white, ribbed silk-taffeta gives the curtains in the new hall a gentle but irregular 'crunchiness', which provides an interesting contrast to the sophisticated design of the painted pelmet.

curtains and drapery

The rooms' relatively low ceilings preclude any elaborately swagged pelmets at the windows, and for the most part I've stuck to the ogee shapes that were there when I came and that follow the lines of the openings. While eschewing fancy fringes, I like to bind the leading edge of curtains in a contrasting colour. I also like to put a narrow band of fabric, almost the colour of the floor itself, along the bottom edge of the curtains, which should touch the floor, but never, ever, puddle. This is a practical as well as subtle refinement, as plain material the colour of the floor won't show up the inevitable bits of the outdoors tracked in from the garden.

The windows in the old part of the house are narrow, so I merely lined the face material with a plain cotton, as interlining would make too much bulk. All these have cartridge-gathered headings, though I prefer to make them fatter than cartridges, more like cigars. In the newer rooms, the curtains are on tracks, either covered with the same material or a bit of wallpaper glued on. As the windows there are wider, the curtains are interlined with 'bump', as it was called when I was young – such a charming word.

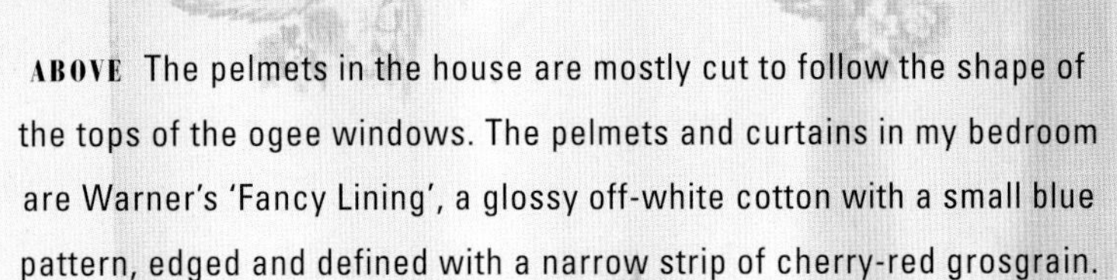

ABOVE The pelmets in the house are mostly cut to follow the shape of the tops of the ogee windows. The pelmets and curtains in my bedroom are Warner's 'Fancy Lining', a glossy off-white cotton with a small blue pattern, edged and defined with a narrow strip of cherry-red grosgrain.

RIGHT, TOP AND BOTTOM In a minute guest bedroom I used a mixture of red stripes – Mauny *papier peint* for the walls, and striped cotton for the bed's corona and the window blind, seen reflected in the mirror – offset by the plain red curtain.

OPPOSITE Antique French chintz and blue 'Fancy Lining', the same as the curtains and again edged with red grosgrain, give my bed a gentle sweep. Edging chintz in a solid colour is an essential touch.

TRANSITIONS

It must have been the most basic of shelters that the original builders put up here in these game-teeming forests; they chose a wide clearing, hard by a narrow stream, to pause and rest and revive.

What is particularly interesting, and perhaps unique, is that the basic style of that earliest construction has clearly influenced successive generations, so that the nature of the architecture has thereafter retained a flavour of the period before. The eighteenth-century ogee-arched windows and doors echo the former Jacobean taste. No Neoclassical pavilion was erected in its place when its surrounding parkland was re-landscaped in Capability Brown Romanticism; no chalet-like excrescence tacked on to its symmetrical façade by overzealous millionaire hotshots.

So the house has dictated its various inhabitants' additions, the most thorough of these being, in the 1950s, the wood-boarded 'Elm Cottage' added by John Fowler behind the minute former stables, which were transformed into a library. Sensitively designed by the architect Philip Jebb and invisible from garden frontage, this muted grey timber construction sinks imperceptibly into the backcloth of towering trees, while the new entrance hall, a sturdy square of wood blocks resembling stone, gives an appealing solidity to those arriving, and is similarly almost unseen from the pale brick façade.

These neatly executed additions are internally so in keeping with the feel of the house that the pull of using Gothic furniture and decorative elements is one I am happy to find irresistible. I like the rooms to flow harmoniously from one to another, uniting the various transitions from the house's inception to the present day.

OPPOSITE Looking from the dining room, with its serene, cool shades of fresh green and grey, through to the warm, red-toned library. The beams on the ceiling mark the divisions of the stalls for the horses when this room was the stables. On the left is a cupboard on a stand in the Strawberry Hill Gothic taste. I have often copied the pierced doors as fronts to mask audio-visual impedimenta, like speakers.

JAMES GIBBS

DAVID BAILEY
ANTONIO

OPPOSITE Muted pinks and soft reds and yellows are sharpened by bright-coloured books and a china pomegranate found in a Turkish tourist trap. The model torso is alabaster and the framed note behind it is a letter of praise from the great Nancy Lancaster – praise indeed.

RIGHT On the walls of the red-striped bedroom – here seen from the hallway, with its bold, gold floral Mauny wallpaper – hang original architectural drawings by the great architect Edwin Lutyens. Beneath the Swedish chair is a horse blanket bought from my local saddler, used as a rug.

BELOW Looking from the hall into the pale pink guest bathroom in the main house, where the walls are massed with eighteenth-century sepia engravings. I first saw a room decorated like this in Biddick Hall, the Lambton house outside Durham.

Each room in the house has a distinct character of its own and a very different but subtle union. One glides seamlessly from one room into the next, a colour or a pattern echoed or emphasized, the transition smooth and yet surprising.

FURNITURE

Though the emphasis on the Gothic style of furniture is evident throughout the house, it is not the only one by any means. The great joy of these rooms is that they seem to embrace anything, from classically proportioned stuff to the downright kitsch, and everything seems to meld together.

All the things I've found over the years, including the pieces of furniture, 'talk' to each other comfortingly. Because the rooms are so small, the eye travels fast around them, without ever having to stop and go, 'Wow! That's a special piece'. Obviously, the scale of pieces has to be restricted here, but my way around that has been to find certain bits for each room which, because of their simple, clean lines, appear bigger than they are. This gives a sturdy geometric foundation to build on, to be surrounded by the fussier, funnier stuff that gives the rooms an interesting jolt. And usually these bigger items are pale in colour, whether that's the surface of a table massed with objects, or the soft gleam of upholstery on a sofa spiked with great splashy flowers.

In general, I keep flooring – except where there are old, wonky terracotta tiles – pale as well, to create a neutral backdrop for the furniture that sits on it. It's an odd fact of life that almost any flooring, especially carpets, 'read' almost white – something to do with the light falling on them – especially if you half-shut your eyes, though blacks or

OPPOSITE The faux panelling by George Oakes in the entrance hall provides linear contrast to the curved form of a white-painted console table with later-added twiddles. I kept meaning to remove them, but I've grown to love them.

OPPOSITE The 'concert' fauteuil in the old hall is covered with taupe-coloured ultrasuede. The cushion is a scrap of early Aubusson tapestry.

ABOVE Red and black horsehair on a Regency Gothic chair in the staircase hall, which also houses the all-important drinks trolley sandwiched between simple bookcases.

RIGHT One of a pair of William IV cane armchairs in the red library, surrounded by more bookshelves. The painting on the top shelf is by my beloved friend Romana McEwen. As you can tell, I like cushions to be floppy, not overstuffed.

navy blues (perish the thought) tend to soak it up. On these carpets you can chuck any old thing – bits of seen-better-days Savonneries (the knotted-pile carpets, both Continental and English) or Oriental rugs, and I often use American-Indian tribal saddle blankets.

The point is that all of these must always look washed out and worn in. The best kilims have usually been scrubbed in azure Turkish seas and left to fade in the sun – there is nothing more jarring than those shrieking chemical colours in the ghastly things that people haul home from Morocco or India. On the other hand, a really jazz-bright, flat-weave rug, such as the one in my red library, fizzes up a dark room.

Greens and greys of varying intensity are the immediate impression in the dining room. Then the details kick in – the delicate foliage on the painted walls, the sable stab of exotic birds and bugs, and the stronger forms and colours of the furniture.

ABOVE A painted Gothic side chair in my dining room blends in well with the painted walls. The eighteenth-century French column next to it, and the large urn that sits on top of it, bring a majestic scale to the small room.

OPPOSITE In the same room, a rather more comfortable dining chair, one of eight, upholstered in Pierre Frey's 'Ming' china bowl material, which I sprayed with tea to deaden the white background. I prefer armchairs in dining rooms; these are reproduction cheapies, their frames now silvered. The butch Rococo sideboard at the right was a small table, until I sawed it in half to make a pair. The other half is in the garden room.

OPPOSITE Two huge wooden 'books' on a cabriole-legged base hold forgotten-about clippings and photographs in the library. The bright-coloured rug is a Kandinsky-inspired cotton one from India, picked up in Spitalfields Market.

ABOVE LEFT An amusing tripod Gothic-style side table from the early 1960s is edged with faux bamboo and has a geranium-red fringe painted above its quatrefoil, in the garden room.

ABOVE RIGHT In the pink bathroom an NH Design occasional table is painted white with randomly placed dots, which give it more character. I often paint furniture with spots such as these.

I consciously avoid the mix-and-match trap. It's more like mismatch and muddle with me. I suppose there is a sort of basic colour palette in each room, but after that, almost anything goes.

The strong, sculptural shapes of table and chair legs are offset and softened by the use of fabric. For example, the two low slipper chairs in my sitting room have been upholstered with gathered ruffles that reach to the ground, anchoring them. I almost always choose patterned cotton, chintz or a small print for this kind of upholstery, but here, I haven't dressed the pair of chairs in the same uniform, as having them different looks more relaxed, less contrived. In the red library, on the other hand, a low chair is covered with a bit of old toile de Jouy printed with pastoral vignettes in sludgy mauve-brown, a shade I love, as it harmonizes with all other colours.

Occasional tables are either covered with pretty cloths or they get a playful, dotty decorative treatment, often literally dots spotted on irregularly, which somehow relieves the tension. I simply love painted furniture, and I even slap coats of white paint on boring mahogany or oak pieces to make them live and breathe.

LEFT On the staircase landing a small folding circular table, bought years ago from a dealer who was alleged to be a bastard royal, holds a plaster bust of Louis XVIII below a portrait of a Venetian noblewoman feeding biscuits to her spaniel. This picture was found by Geoffrey Scott for my father, and used to hang on the stairs at Great Hundridge Manor. The perky toy dog under the table is, in fact, an Edwardian nightclothes holder.

ABOVE Another plaster bust of an aristocratic gent stands on a typically French console table in the entrance hall. Behind him is a tall, painted Regency looking glass that was also at Hundridge.

OPPOSITE A detail of the console table. Its fine carving had traces of gilding when I got it, but I prefer it painted the colour my parents called Elephant's Breath – a great 1930s colour.

There is something magical about running one's fingers over carved elements of antique furniture. One thinks with wonder of the craftsmen who created such classically informed, evocative details.

ABOVE For the top of this table I made a frame of green-painted batons and then glued sepia Russian tiles inside it. Then I 'marbleized' the edge with a black Magic Marker. The whole process took less than an hour.

RIGHT Here is the same table, standing in front of the window in the dining room that looks out to the woods. The hand-painted geometric border on the patterned curtains was getting pretty frail, so I moved them to the far side of the window and use the plain middle ones, in cream slub linen, for pulling. The lamp on the table is a tin basket of spiky tin dahlias. They are very aggressive and a nightmare to move.

ABOVE The painted Gothic cupboard-on-stand in the dining room holds glassware. Its little oak-leaf fastening is exactly the kind of detail I find irresistible.

ABOVE RIGHT A bust of Alexander Pope peers over the crenellated cornice of the cupboard. Under it is a French fireside chair, with a cushion made from a scrap of fiendishly expensive Lyonnais leopard-skin silk velvet.

OPPOSITE A crane strolls next to the delightfully unconvincing palm tree's dusty pink pot behind the Rococo half-console, which I suppose is Italian and one of a pair that act as sideboards. In the centre of the table is a painted tôle vase with tulip-shaped holders for candles; you can jam any old flowers into it and they look enchanting, especially when the candles are lit for dinner. The black butterflies appear to be attracted by the metal urn lamps, which have shades made from oddments of toile de Jouy.

While I don't studiously look for Gothic furniture, the house calls out for it, and I can barely resist – the cupboard in the dining room exemplifies my passion, down to its little carved oak-leaf catch, the sort of detail that makes it look so special.

CLASSICAL ELEMENTS

One of the blessings of European culture is that there are no restrictions on using human or animal forms in interior decoration, as some religions proscribe. One can get pretty fed up with endlessly repeated foliage and interlaced patterns.

I have a theory that the earliest shape of panelling – rounded corners with inward curves at the top, bottom and sides – was originally derived from the hides of bison or some such, which prehistoric man would have tacked up in his wood hut to keep out the arctic wind. Then, when the art of tapestry weaving was discovered, but wall hangings could only be woven with a straight edge, the panels became square or rectangular to contain them. Indoor heating did away with these coverings, and panelling became the thing we know today.

OPPOSITE The bust of Louis XVIII in my staircase hall in close-up. When he fled France, he lived not so far away from here at Hartwell House in Buckinghamshire. I love his crisp cravat and sash and epaulettes. In the portrait that hangs above him, you can see the name of the Venetian lady depicted on the folder on the table. She is Laudiga Camilla Ronca Morici Fabiano, or perhaps Fabiano was the artist?

GREGOR VON REZZORI
THE SNOWS OF YESTERYEAR
ORDINARY THUNDERSTORMS
ELIA KAZAN
KAZAN ON DIRECTING

ABOVE In the entrance hall a Continental terracotta figure of the Virgin bearing a wheat sheaf and a child stands on a plinth I designed.

ABOVE A later English version of the Virgin and Child, again in terracotta, in the trellis bedroom. The chest of drawers was made by Gillows for my father's family house in Bolton.

Equally, busts and statues must originally have been representations of gods or totems, and gradually they were brought inside as decorative elements. Thank the Lord, as few things make such a bold punctuation mark as a figure or bust or urn, well positioned and lit. I have several busts of my various heroes – especially Marie Antoinette and her circle – that were created at a time when the portrait-bust was at its zenith, but I prefer them in terracotta, or white plaster, as shiny marble is too harsh, too grand, for these surroundings. Moss and lichen-covered, weathered-stone urns bring a touch of the garden into the house. I've even had some casts of iron outdoor urns made in fibreglass for easy, and regular, repositioning.

ABOVE A delightfully lichened stone urn on a small chest made for a grand yacht, with a pair of early Irish silver candlesticks – you can turn them upside down and they become drinking vessels. On the left is a watercolour of the aesthete Stephen Tennant 'in Shelley costume' by Rex Whistler. On the right is Michael Leonard's exquisite drawing of my Pekingese, Zephyr, as an Elizabethan lady in a ruff. It's postcard size, and Michael put sixpence in one corner; the framer asked me, 'Shall I rub the price off this postcard?'

Tuesday 8th May
Cocktails Dinner

OPPOSITE An amber-washed bust of a Frenchman wearing the Order of the Golden Fleece stands behind a group of white objects on a table in my sitting room – the three in front are made of paper and were given to me by David Hicks. An invitation to a party in Venice from David Oliver, owner of the Paint Library, is held by a plaster repro of Michelangelo's *David*. We call this 'the David table'.

RIGHT Houdon's portrait-bust of Marie Antoinette is a contemporary casting. I have a portrait of her lover, Count Axel von Fersen, in the old hall next door. Sometimes I show them to each other and their eyes light up with happiness.

There isn't always rhyme or reason to where things go – I often just jumble them together and hope they make a pleasing whole.

Another thing I love is architectural models made of white card or plaster, or even plastic and Lucite, which one can pick up in touristy shops anywhere from Istanbul to St Petersburg. Among the most pleasure-giving things in the Royal Academy Summer Exhibition is the room devoted to architectural maquettes. Seeing them, I always wish I had the technical skill to make such enchanting objects myself. Casts of hands and feet or facial features are also pleasingly interesting objects to display and can be found in museum shops all over the place.

ART AND MEMORIES

I believe almost anything looks good when it is framed well. I was lucky enough to inherit a few pictures from my parents, but I can't pretend they are in any way great 'art', which, in any case, I don't particularly respond to. And, of course, they are all imbued with memories.

The portrait of my mother – and it's not an overflattering likeness – used to hang in an obscure corner at Hundridge, despite the fact that it was greatly admired when exhibited at the Royal Academy Summer Show. I can vividly remember her wearing the dress and hat when she came from a sitting to pick me up from my first-ever school. The oil-green bow was added later, and afterwards always lay in a glass bowl on her dressing table, dusty with her powder. I wish there was the space to put a picture light below as well as above her portrait, as was done in the eighteenth century, the time when her ancestors were the major players in Whig society. But that would mean moving the grog tray – an unthinkable idea – and anyway, she is almost within toasting distance of the painting I found by chance of her family's country villa, Bessborough House at Roehampton. I had no idea this exquisite building, by William Chambers who went on to design Somerset House and many temples and the pagoda at Kew Gardens, still existed. After several years of wild-goose chase, I discovered it is now called Parkstead House and stands in all its relatively untouched glory overlooking Richmond Park.

OPPOSITE A portrait of my mother, Diana Ponsonby, painted by Robin Guthrie in 1948 – it was shown at the Royal Academy that year – hangs above the drinks trolley (she would have approved of that) in the staircase hall. The glasses, ravishingly engraved, are part of a set I bought in a house sale in Ascot. Behind is a bargee's bailing bucket I use as an ice pail. The bitters are Peychaud's, from New Orleans, the best in the world. I stock up whenever I go there.

REX WHISTLER
Jonathan Swift / Rex Whistler / Gulliver's Travels / Herbert
THE LIFE OF NOEL COWARD
COLE LESLEY
MICHAEL WISHART
BLOND & BRIGGS
SELINA HASTINGS
JOHN MURRAY
A CHILDHOOD IN SCOTLAND
TWO STORIES & A MEMORY
THE LAST LEOPARD
by James Morris
PAX Britannica
PAX Britannica
FABER
A Life of Contrasts
DIANA MOSLEY
James Lees-Milne
DEEP ROMANTIC CHASM
James Lees-Milne
BENEATH A WANING MOON
JOHN BETJEMAN
EXTRA DRY
DRICK'S
GIN

ABOVE LEFT A late eighteenth-century painting of the Ponsonby family's villa at Roehampton, Bessborough House, by Luke Sullivan, hangs above the chopping board in the kitchen. I found it at Sotheby's years ago. I had no idea the house still existed, but it does, untouched and as designed by William Chambers, as part of the University of Roehampton.

ABOVE RIGHT Engravings of 'Bonnie' Prince Charles Edward Stuart, 'the Young Pretender' (shown here), and his brother, the Duke of York, hang on either side of the front door in the entrance hall. I am always amazed by the finesse and delicacy of eighteenth-century engravings, and have several dotted around, preferably portraits with some link to the historical characters I specially admire. Their classic black frames with a narrow gold slip give a subdued dignity to the intricate mayhem they surround.

OPPOSITE Ordnance Survey maps, various documents pertaining to the house and some royal letters hang against an overscaled 'damask' wallpaper by George Spencer, in the downstairs loo. I bought the beadwork Chinoiserie lantern from Cecil Beaton's sale at Broadchalke. I loved it when I stayed with him and was lucky to be able to afford it as a memento of that dear man.

ORDNANCE SURVEY
Scale 1:10 560 or 6 Inches to 1 Mile
HOOK
ODIHAM
SHEET SU 75 SW
MY COPY OF NICKY HASLAM'S BOOK HAS A CUTE LITTLE LEATHER JACKET!
'SPECTATOR' 14 NOV 2009
CLARENCE HOUSE
29th January, 2006
SHEET SU75

ABOVE A motley crew, including some of my favourite people, on the mantelpiece of the sitting room fireplace. Among them are Terry Kramer and Lee Radziwill, with Paolo Moschino on the far right. The photograph of me by James Ostrer, done to look like a Lucian Freud painting, was in a National Portrait Gallery exhibition. Four small crystal vases on plinths hold one budding rose, but any old flower looks wonderful in them. The cupcakes are, in fact, egg timers. When lit, the pair of nineteenth-century French candlesticks, as used by every student at that time, illuminate the delicate landscape behind the flying figure of St Joseph (who can't be seen here) and a very fanciful view of Copertino, which is, in fact, a tiny village in Puglia in the south of Italy.

I'll frame up almost anything that appeals, even postcards (but never photographs). Often, if I buy a small original by a lesser, romantic artist, such as Martin Battersby, I'll frame a reproduction of his work to make a pair if needed. Battersby did a series of mural capriccios for Lady Diana Cooper's Château de St Firmin outside Paris, so these pictures, and the tiny painting of Diana in *The Miracle* by her mother, the Duchess of Rutland, remind me constantly of her beloved, erudite and beautiful daughter.

Letters, or large-scale local Ordnance Survey maps, add piquancy to even the smallest rooms, while photographs of favourite friends and other trivia hobnob on the sitting-room mantelshelf, the only one in the house wide enough, perhaps luckily, to take all this personal memorabilia.

CREATING TABLEAUX

While the grouping of objects into tableaux – or 'tablescapes', as David Hicks deftly named them – can often look contrived, in my case they are pretty haphazard. I suddenly realize that I've got a lot of things of vaguely one colour, or theme, and that they would look happier put together in a group.

Sadly, or perhaps not, I don't have a mass of Louis XV gold boxes, or valuable bronzes, or delicate porcelain. More likely, bits and pieces picked up at random, and often moved from one theme park to another where they jog along together. A brown wax bust of actor Rotrou, a naïve portrait of Lucian Freud and a drawing by Eric Gill are learning to share a console tabletop in the recently redecorated garden room, soon to be joined, I feel sure, by other bits from other places. On the other hand, in my sitting room another bust, of Marie Antoinette, gazes, serenely silhouetted, before a background of sepia engravings and drawings. The one bang behind her, an Italian 'old master' ink sketch, has 'From Chatsworth' written on the back, though I don't hold any high hopes of this for security in old age.

OPPOSITE On a console in the garden room is a large portrait-bust of Louis XIV's court actor Rotrou by Caffieri, made in wax to get his client's approval before carving the marble. Behind him is the reflection of a wood chandelier designed by John Fowler. I found the painting of Lucian Freud in one of the art booths along the railings on Piccadilly. A pair of spotted wood appliqué light fittings – the candles spotted as well – and the china lamp create dramatic shadows at night-time.

ABOVE The dinky yacht commode is just the right depth for the narrow old hall. Above it is a portrait I found at Christie's in South Kensington. Lucy Ferry took one look and said, 'That's my uncle!' Maybe it is because the sitter looks like her son, my godson Otis Ferry, that it caught my eye.

RIGHT The stone-topped console in the old hall where my visitors' book lives is a typical example of found, collected and inherited things. An ink self-portrait by Cecil Beaton reminds me daily of that dear, brilliant friend. David Hockney gave me the landscape sketch when demonstrating his *cire perdue*, or lost wax, technique. Lucian Freud's engraving *After Chardin* is, perhaps, the most valuable thing I own and have treasured since the day he came to lunch with it. The set of French ormolu candlesticks of the seasons belonged to my parents. Behind the glass battery-tank holding crab-apple boughs and yellow daisies is James Wyatt's floor plan for the house that 'a grateful nation' proposed to build for the Duke of Wellington, to be called the Palace of Waterloo; it was going to be bigger than Versailles. The Duke refused.

OVERLEAF Marie Antoinette surrounded by French and Italian sepia engravings of old master drawings, which exactly match the wall colour in the sitting room. The whole lot cost about a fiver, but I framed them up 'grand' in rubbed gilt, giving a touch of reflective glitter. The little picture was picked up in Budapest and I lugged the pottery vase back from Portofino.

LEFT Cool creams and whites on the table in the old hall in front of a pair of hurricane lamps. I love this form of ethereal lighting and can't have too many of them.

BELOW Overblown roses from the garden echo the floral motifs on the stripes of Mauny wallpaper on my bedroom wall. The elaborately decorated porcelain vase with vignettes of children playing was found in a Bordeaux junk shop.

OPPOSITE 'Hot' flowers in a faux bois pail stand on a red lacquer chest in the library. The china figure of Garibaldi was given to me by the legendary beauty Lady Diana Cooper, a beloved friend all my life.

floral displays

Flowers play an essential role, partly to enliven the rooms and partly from the sheer pleasure of thinking up new ways to utilize anything growing in the immediate surroundings. I love massed, untidy bouquets of things in season, and try to keep the room's colour scheme in mind so that the arrangement doesn't shriek, 'Look at me'. Alternatively, one whopping great sculptural branch or bough – apple blossom in spring, silver birch (the only 'wild' tree that doesn't wilt when picked) in summer, clusters of golden crab apples in autumn and tall stems of black-flowered ivy in winter. The other day I lopped off the crown of a rogue hawthorn, studded with scarlet berries, for the red library. It only lasted a few days, but it looked terrific. With overscaling like this, I add single perfect blooms straight from the garden, in tiny containers, all over the place. Their very simplicity makes them intrinsically interesting.

Garibaldi

Tuesday 8th M

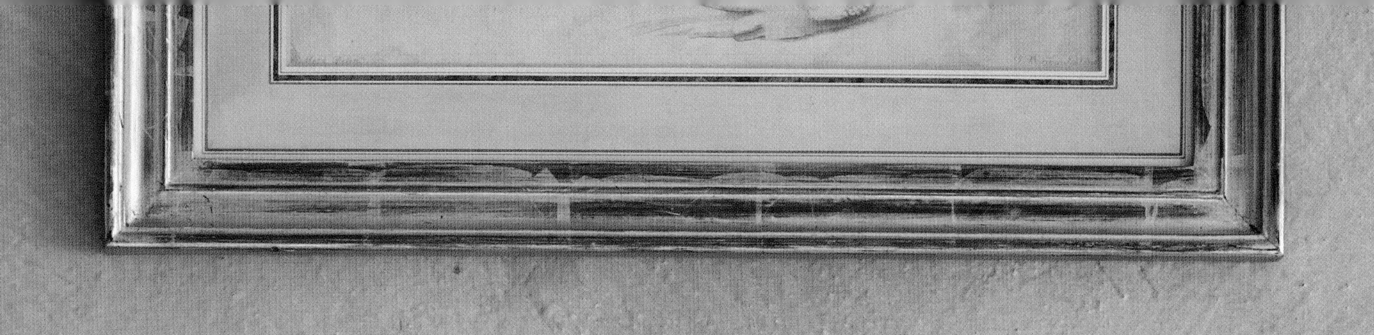

A HOUSE FOR ALL SEASONS

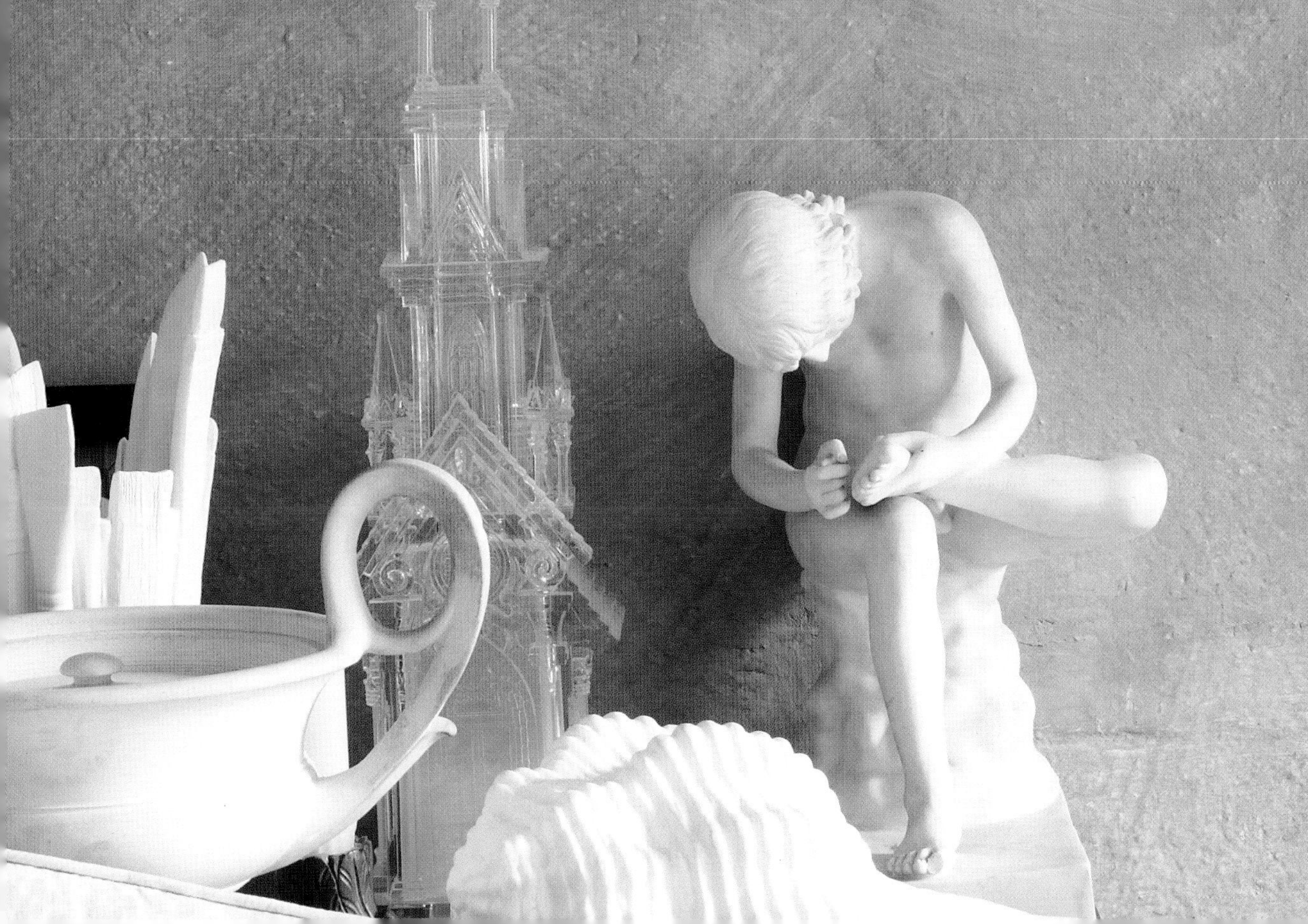

DO COME IN

The arrival point is a surprising contrast to the gabled skyline of the house when approached through the trees, either from the drive or looking up from the lake. It is a sturdy little pavilion, which seems almost unconnected to the actual folly, as its architecture is beefily classical and, despite its size, quite imposing.

Painted tubs containing clipped box trees hint at the formality of the 'green' garden beyond, while the finely carved white Georgian door surround has an inviting air, ideal for greeting guests as their cars crunch the gravel of the circular drive – or, indeed, for waving goodbye. To the left of the front door, a bank of camellias, all linear lace in winter's snows, shyly unfurl their stripes of pink and white and red once winter's frosts are forgotten, to linger as showy saucers. (They were planted in imported soil, as, mercifully, shrubs of the rhododendron family won't grow naturally here, though they do on the acidic soil just across the canal.) By then the Amelanchier tree above them will sway with flocks of bluetits, and the mulberry tree beyond begins its fresh canopy of shade-giving leaves that harbour a horseshoe bat or two, which swoop and squeak as dusk falls.

OPPOSITE The front hall of the Hunting Lodge is the last addition to the original house. A square pavilion with a pyramidal tiled roof, it is seemingly constructed in stone, but in fact these are wood blocks imitating masonry. The door surround is classically English and the lanterns are equally classic Colefax and Fowler.

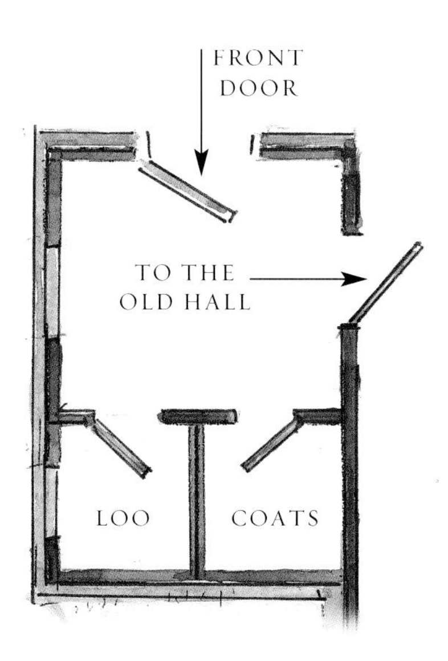

The simple building was the last one to be added by John Fowler, and a necessity, as formerly the front door opened immediately into the old hall, and I imagine the draught was something terrific. I like to think of him standing in the doorway as his celebrated clients like Debo Devonshire or the Pembrokes drew up to be greeted by his quizzical smile and promise of a nifty Bloody Mary. One of his early assistants, Nina Campbell, told me recently that, even before he came to live here, their nickname for John was 'Folly' Fowler – never can the saying 'if the glove fits' have been more appropriate.

Across the threshold, the painted panels of the new hall seem suffused with

RIGHT Inside, the hall feels like a miniature French country house. The doors are picked out with a yellowy grey wash and the skirtings are 'marbleized'. The tall looking glass is typically English, and the portrait-bust in front of it is a rather grumpy-looking old French geezer. The hurricane lanterns have been electrified so they don't blow out when the door is opened.

insubstantial light, now and then tinged palest green, the reflection of lawn and leaves on the dust-coloured panelling. Discreet doors on each side of the console lead to two supreme essentials, the coat cupboard (which also houses many other half-remembered stowaways) and the downstairs loo. Here, after two especially snowy winters caused a leak, I ditched the original small-patterned paper for one with a socking-great scale, and the whole room expanded visually. The actual lav is Westminster by Imperial Bathrooms, the prettiest-shaped one I've ever come across.

Electrified hurricane lamps light this hall at night with candle-power softness, just enough to stop people from tripping over the trugs that hold the wherewithal for a sudden burst of garden-tending enthusiasm. Opposite, under a number of engravings (so suitable for a hallway) are a couple of white-painted Gothic chairs covered in the same material as – and thus a foretaste for – the curtains in the old hall next door, an almost unnoticeable visual link that makes small seem larger.

OPPOSITE The plinth was a prototype I designed for a major commission. It is based on those at Sanssouci, the former summer palace of Frederick the Great, King of Prussia, in Potsdam. The off-white silk curtains reflect light onto the simple, polished oak floorboards.

RIGHT This Gothic chair is covered in Colefax and Fowler's 'Oak Leaf' fabric. A hidden cupboard is masked by an engraving of my great-great-great-grandfather, the second Earl of Bessborough. A diplomat and founder member of the Dilettante Society, he was reputedly the lover of Princess Amelia, the daughter of George II.

OPPOSITE Count Axel von Fersen, 'the handsomest man in Europe', peers over Napoleon. I bought this portrait from the collection of Evangeline Bruce, who wrote about both of these legendary ladykillers. The Colefax and Fowler 'Oak Leaf' curtains are edged with a strip of golden yellow rep. The pelmets have been cut to echo the shape of the windows.

ABOVE LEFT A model of the Vendôme Column in Paris is topped by a figure of Napoleon, who removed that of Louis XIV and installed himself.

ABOVE RIGHT Nicely wonky terracotta tiles get a weekly buffing by Jean Major, my wonderful housekeeper.

THE OLD HALL

The old hall is long and narrow, though it must have been a bit shorter until the house was added to. But with windows on three walls – all different, I might add, and a nightmare to unite, curtain-wise – it's as ungloomy as a hall can be. Even so, the room comes into its own on winter evenings, with the flames from crackling logs dancing a reflection on the terracotta tiles. People always use it as a spillover from the sitting room, and cluster snugly on the club fender and on the (fake) fur-thrown sofa opposite. I'm forced to say these are about the only places they can sit, as the other chairs have become easels for as yet unplaced drawings – one of a rather dour house façade, said to have been done by none other than Capability Brown.

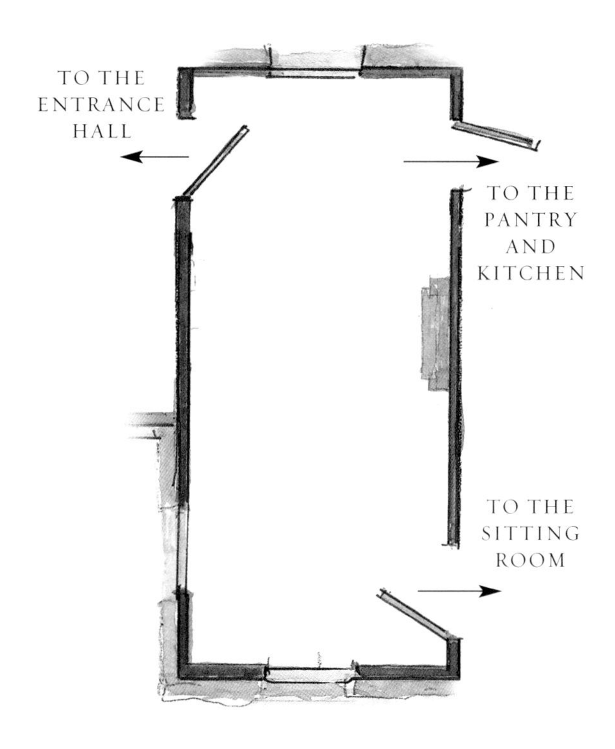

OVERLEAF The faux-panelled old hall; you can see how narrow the room is. The club fender is Edwardian and was a perfect fit. James Wyatt's architectural 'slips' for the outbuildings of the Palace of Waterloo hang opposite. The metal pyramid money box in the foreground was given to me, as were many other treasures, by my friend Christopher Butterworth, the best *antiquaire* in Pimlico. The lampshades are antique pleated Mauny wallpaper.

LEFT I have so many architectural drawings that I have no space to hang them. Chairs have to double up as easels.

ABOVE This window is beside the faux door I have just made outside (see page 23). A portfolio of office memos from my boss at American *Vogue*, Diana Vreeland, sits on the windowsill and brings back constant memories of that heady time in New York.

Before I bit the bullet and made a proper dining room in Elm Cottage, we would eat here, as did John Fowler. But the effort of lugging all the books off the round table before meals, and back after, let alone de-picturing the chairs, got the better of me. Now the table groans under ever-growing piles of massive tomes – as it's only made of chipboard, I live in fear of it giving up the ghost at any moment.

In warm weather, the old hall is really more of a passage to the sitting room and garden door. People can stop and sign the visitors' book, which lies on the side table. 'Have you got a pen?' Why doesn't somebody design these books with an irremovable one? And with real ink, of course.

a relaxing firelit warmer

There are fires and fires, but this one positively eats logs for breakfast. By the time one trudges in from an ear-chilling afternoon walk, almost the entire contents of two log baskets have been sacrificed to its greedy maw. Still, wet-weather gear and Wellingtons (appropriate, as Wyatt's designs for the Iron Duke's self-rejected palace hang all around) are bone-dry before you can say Jack Robinson, or more likely Robinsons Lemon Barley Water, which, mixed with a good slug of Scotch to wash down a wedge of buttered fruit cake, is just the ticket before a pre-dinner nap.

ABOVE LEFT The little picture on the end table that I designed is a pair of fanciful sphinxes by Martin Battersby. I like tables that have a low rim around the edge, so things can't be pushed off.

ABOVE RIGHT AND RIGHT All the necessities for a hot whisky toddy ready by the fire for when I return from a tramp along the old canal by the lake. The Edwardian fender, brass-banistered and topped with battered leather, is the ideal place for sudden warmth when taking off one's Wellingtons on a frosty evening.

MAKE YOURSELF COMFORTABLE

As a place to relax and read, or in which to gather friends together, the sitting room must exude comfort and ease, above all else. It needs to be a warm and welcoming room, inviting guests to rest, to while away the evening with conversation and conviviality.

This room – the main, if minute, sitting room in the oldest part of the house – encapsulates the essence of the way I like a country room to be: informal, calm, colourful and comfortable. The door leads directly from the garden, so, as there is nothing more boring than making guests take off their shoes, a 'dirt'-coloured hair-cord carpet covers the floor. Comfort, however, like beauty, is in the mind of the beholder. If a chair or sofa looks comfortable, it will be. The eighteenth century saw to that, creating comfortable furniture for every occasion and profession. The current fad for spiky hardness is fine if you don't want people to sit around for too long – hotels and restaurants come to mind – or if you positively don't like your guests. Height is all-important. Low and deep sofas may seem cool, but they are hell to sit in, let alone get up from. Better, in this house, to plump for time-tested shapes

OPPOSITE The sitting room, barely 3.7m (12ft) square, has to be deeply inviting and comfortable. Tan lampshades give a golden light in the evening. In front of the fire, as a coffee table, stands a low Victorian bench upholstered in petit point, which took me years to complete. It depicts a stylized interpretation of the gabled skyline of the façade of the Hunting Lodge in the same muddy green as in the fabrics on the slipper chairs and tables, with a background in the same shade of pink as the walls. I love a white shag hearth rug. All mine are flokatis from Greece; they're cheap as chips, so you can just bin them when they're past it.

SMALL PERIOD GARDENS
ROY STRONG
COUNTRY GARDENS

I love small rooms, especially in the country, when one can open them up to the sunlight outside, or make them snug and warm with a roaring fire. I like a country room to be related to, and yet distinctly different from, the garden.

and heights, not too squidgy, with comforting cushioning for the back and a few loose cushions to wedge into place for essential support, not put there for mere décor.

The sofas in the sitting room have been with me for nearly 40 years and have never even needed re-covering. The heavy, slightly sheened cotton seems to shed mud and dog hairs, and over time has settled into inviting non-crispness. The slipper chairs, in much thinner stuff, have had to have new covers. I made the mistake of sending the old ones, which had shrunk, to be copied and, of course, the new ones are a bit too small and tight. The shaggy white hearth rug partly conceals the fact that they don't quite touch the ground – but, live and learn.

The irregularly plastered walls were originally painted with a time-remembered recipe of bull's blood and distemper, which produces the subtlest shade of pink-brown. This soft colour gives a complexion-flattering glow, especially at night when the buff card-shaded lamps are lit. Subdued light upwards but bright pools below, for reading, are ideal for looks and ease; and with everything at hand – books, ashtrays, matches, a poker set, drinks – to enhance this desirable ambiance, the room is comforting as well as comfortable.

OPPOSITE, TOP LEFT I bought this little pastel as the sitter looks like Cecil Beaton. Behind it is one of a – rather good – pair of Chinese lamps that have travelled with me from New York to Arizona to Los Angeles to London and now here. Commemorative medals and a cut-glass obelisk given to me by my friend Lynn Barber clutter the tabletop.

OPPOSITE, TOP RIGHT I like to use bits of antique china as ashtrays, though it's getting harder and harder to find the odd piece. The black metal, gold-inlaid pomegranate is Turkish, and the pile of white books, actually a light, came from the shop in the Louvre in Paris.

OPPOSITE, BELOW In the sitting room, the white wall-cupboard in the corner was for keeping bread warm. The picture over the fire is of St Joseph of Copertino, the patron saint of aviation. Known as 'The Flying Monk', it belonged to my father. St Joseph is the patron saint of levitation and, therefore, flying, and as such he is the patron saint of the Royal Air Force, which was pointed out to me by the Commander of RAF Odiham nearby. That's the kind of sideways coincidence I find ever-fascinating about furnishing rooms.

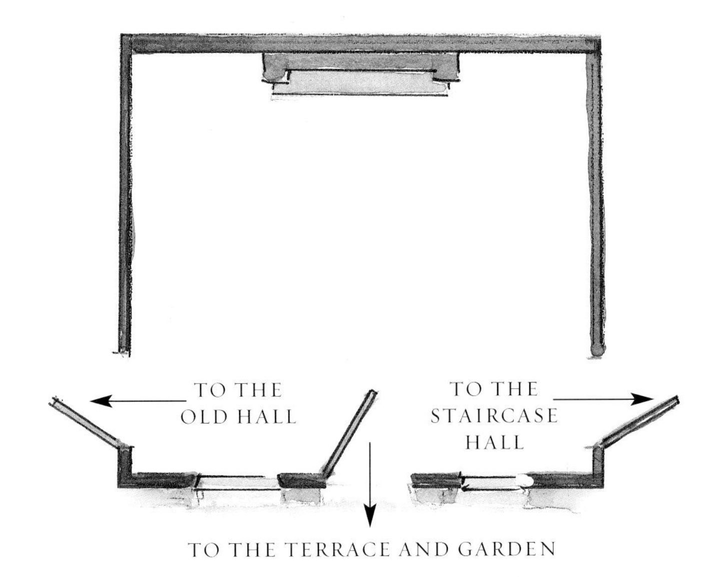

See you
Soon
enjoy the
MORPHINE
Love
THE Erotic
Print Society
SUPERIOR SHIP TIME
HORTUS 87
HORTUS 82

I never buy anything purely for its value. I like possessions that smile back at me.

OPPOSITE In a German porcelain bowl is a pile of plastic crayfish, which were part of a table décor we did for Cartier. A get-well letter from Lucian Freud is propped up behind a postcard stuck with sequins from my closest friend Min Hogg.

ABOVE RIGHT This photograph of the Hunting Lodge at the turn of the century was found by Sheila Millard, Odiham's archivist. The little painting of one of the pavilions just after the great storm of 1987 was done by the American decorator Mark Hampton. The sketch just seen at the back is by Prince Charles, done on a menu at the Duke of York's wedding.

RIGHT I found the Perspex fantasy tower in a Moscow toy shop. Bits of anything white surround it on the 'David' table.

OVERLEAF The overscaled sofas flanking the fire form an enticing seating area, surrounded by a multitude of favourite objects found over the years. Photograph albums pile up under the needlework stool, with the latest books on top, including my own. The black graphite feather was given to me by Hannah Rothschild when I completed my autobiography.

Philip de Laszlo
A LIFE OF PICASSO

LEFT There's nothing better than an ice-cold Martini to start off a sociable evening. Gin, of course, not Vodka – that's a Vodka Martini.

BELOW My mother silently approves the preparation of the evening's tipple.

OPPOSITE Here you can see the exquisite detail of the vine-leaf engraving on this 1930s glassware. Extremely delicate, it's not used very often and is a total stranger to the dishwasher.

evening cocktails

Whenever I have guests for dinner, I like to kick off proceedings with cocktails in the sitting room. There's nothing like the snap of an ice-cold Dry Martini in front of the fire in any season, especially when it's made with Sacred Gin, a miraculous spirit created by Ian Hart, who distills a few bottles a week in his private microdistillery in London's Highgate. Ian has also started to make his own English Vermouth, which has a herbal bouquet and taste that knocks the Continental stuff into a cocked hat. Perhaps I should say 'crocked', as after a couple of frosted glassfuls of these concoctions, the world seems distinctly rosier. Thinnest lemon peel is all that's needed, though sometimes I vary the recipe to a Gibson, which I was introduced to by Cole Porter in the 1960s. Tiny, white pearl onions and a smidgen of their juice is the secret – one well worth getting under your belt. Another great year-round cocktail is an Old-Fashioned – a sugar lump soaked in bitters, an orange slice, a slug of Rye topped up with icy soda. Chuck in a maraschino cherry. Nectar.

QUICKSANDS
PAX Britannica
A Life of Contrasts
James Lees-Milne

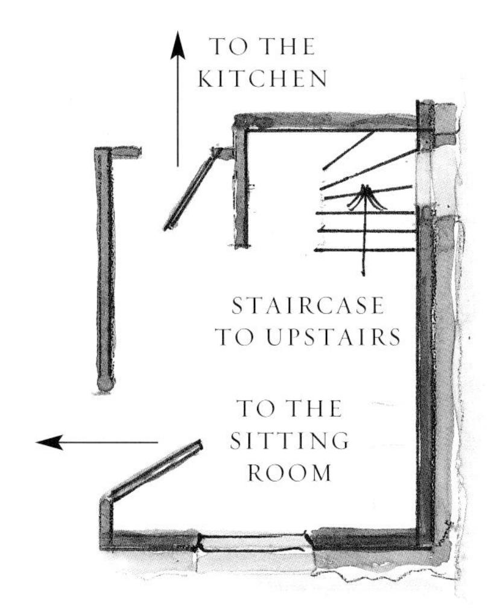

OPPOSITE This little room has many different names. When people want to call out, it's called the telephone room, otherwise it's the staircase hall, or the bar.

RIGHT The Bakelite dial phone was given to me by Paolo Moschino. I love it, but it's a trial to use, as you can't press any buttons when 'those people' ask. The small ink drawing of a gate grille is by Robert Adam the elder.

OVERLEAF, LEFT In the same room, cream faille curtains drape gracefully at the leaded window, with views onto the garden and lake beyond.

OVERLEAF, RIGHT The engraving shows portraits of Louis XIV at various stages of his long life.

THE STAIRCASE HALL

This minuscule space between the sitting room and kitchen is the nerve centre of the house. By that, I mean that you have to hold your nerve when clambering up the steep, narrow staircase that rises off to one side; or when trying, tray-laden, to open the all-too-well-concealed low door that leads to a 'cupboard' crammed haphazardly with hi-fi stuff, which you have to walk through to get to the kitchen. The room itself is mostly bookshelves, where I keep the special memoirs that I constantly re-read, along with the reference books, such as Pevsner, that I like to keep to hand.

PORTRAITS
DE
LOUIS LE GRAND

LE CANZONI DI Sophia Loren
EDITH PIAF

OPPOSITE AND ABOVE Under the stairs, with its dark green handrail and finials, is a strange painting by Martin Battersby. The lead box below it, standing on a rack for LP records, once encased a wooden casket covered and lined with eighteenth-century wallpaper fragments. It had been buried and later dug up. I like to think it contained protestations of undying love, so I keep my great-grandfather's letters to his future wife in it; some are dated 1845.

There is also, of course, the all-important drinks trolley so guests can help themselves, and the now almost-redundant land-line telephone. On the overscale wallpaper, beside the portrait of my mother, hang the engravings and letters of the various King Louis of France, the latter being mostly orders of committal to the Bastille. At this distance in time, they make one shudder a good deal less than their recipients must have done on opening these floridly penned documents.

Beef up the scale of wall coverings in small spaces. The size creates an immediate *coup d'oeil*, pulling everything together, whereas small patterns tend to simply trail away to nothing.

LEFT The silver spoon holder, made to resemble shards of ice, was a present from Luchino Visconti, the film director. Behind it is Lucian Freud's sketch of the whippet belonging to his assistant David Dawson. And behind again, is a painting by Perienne Christian, Lucian's last pupil.

OPPOSITE The library in all its muddle. I have completely run out of bookshelf space in every room, but I quite like the rugged informality of books tucked in any old how.

THE LIBRARY

Considering this room is, in essence, a passage from the old house to the new extension, between more utilitarian areas, such as the kitchen, and the fancifully decorated dining room, it works as an extremely inviting space. People have usually lost their bearings when they initially enter it, exclaiming, 'Oh, this house is much bigger than I thought.' That's one of the pleasures of the place, that each room, however small, is a surprise.

Being red from top to toe, the library has an instantly inviting warmth, conducive to telly-watching and late-night talks, but it also works as an ideal spot for Sunday breakfast with the newspapers and 'The Andrew Marr Show'. The furniture is quite a mishmash, leaning towards comfort rather than looks. Of course, there are the inevitable books, particularly dictionaries and reference books, stacks of magazines and plenty of club-like dark-shaded lamps.

WHO'S WHO
1985
COMPLETE
WORDFINDER
Slang
BEATON
HOUGHTON

LEFT A swing-arm lamp with a tattered brown shade and weird metal bobble fringe lights an octagonal lacquer table that belonged to my parents. The toile de Jouy slipper chair would have been approved of by Elsie Mendl, the American actress and interior decorator, who gazes serenely, surrounded by a cerulean blue background.

ABOVE A tôle lamp with a tôle shade stops any reflection in the television nearby. The Chinese trunk was almost the first thing I bought for my little house in Waterloo in the late 1950s.

OPPOSITE The room in an earlier incarnation – a bit tidier, I notice. I had to cut a hole in a really rather good Oriental carpet to accommodate the post, on which hang two papier-mâché masks for a ball in Venice given by Anouska Hempel. This is the only 'hot' room downstairs and it can take all shades of red. The sofa covering is a cotton version of a velvet-ribbed material that I longed for but couldn't afford at the time.

It's amusing to think that this room was once the demesne's stables for livestock. The large central post – essential, as far as providing support for the roof is concerned – once divided the mangers. I like to imagine a pony stamping its hooves on the frosty cobbles, or a milkmaid perched on a three-legged stool, her cheek resting against a sweet-smelling flank and the daily supply squirting frothily into a tin pail, as I slot the latest series of 'Mad Men' into the DVD player.

WHO'S WHO 1985
Know your Rights
ISLAM

library breakfast

A proper cooked breakfast is a great treat for me, both to make and to munch. Usually it's just yoghurt and coffee, but there's no question that 'a little "eggy" something on a tray', as Noel Coward put it – in bed, for lazybones – can't be beaten. Guests sometimes cajole me into making the real thing, perhaps with a glass of freshly squeezed orange juice, the pick of seasonal fruit and a round of toast with home-made jam. And what better place to have it than in the rosy warmth of the library, snuggled on the sofa with the Sunday papers, the latest magazines or books, and the news on the telly?

ABOVE LEFT AND RIGHT The warm colours and subdued light in the library make it the perfect place for a relaxing and informal weekend breakfast.

RIGHT Queen Elizabeth The Queen Mother once sat on the blue-and-white striped cushion, now on my sofa. I had put it on her chair in the royal box that I had decorated for a ballet gala at Sadler's Wells.

The WOODEN SPOON
COMPANY
CHAUCER
Black Cherry
EXTRA JAM
PREPARED by hand

TABLE MANNERS

Having made this room comparatively recently, out of what were a couple of fairly useless small spaces in the clapboard-clad addition designed by Philip Jebb, I can't think how on earth I did without it for as long as I did.

The only disadvantage to this room is that it is as far from the kitchen as it could be. But at least this means that at the end of a raucous dinner, or Sunday lunch, one can just close the door and forget about it until morning – or at least until the guests have left. I rather dread the politeness of 'Let me help you?' However well intentioned, it only means one has to direct, and redirect, where everything goes. A great advantage of the dining room being a cul-de-sac is that I can do an elaborate table setting that remains a revelation until we 'go through', which is surely the essence of a gala occasion. Added to all this is the fact that the room looks so convivial and uplifting when it's not being used for eating, which is about the only time I tend to put flowers on the table. One day, my wonderful neighbour Princess Joan Aly Khan told me she thought flowers

RIGHT The dining room as it was before I found the 'Ming' china bowls material for the chairs (in, of all places, Vienna). I liked this look for a long time and then began to think it seemed too overtly and too fashionably Gustavian. The French-grey Rococo-style table, with its green-grey faux-marble top, came from a house auction. The tall column was the original stand for the bust of Rotrou, now in the garden room. The urn on top is fibreglass, moulded from an iron one in the garden.

on a table at meals were common – traditionally, their scent was considered to interfere with the aroma of, say, truffles, or to swamp the bouquet of Château Lafite – and her dictum has stuck with me ever since.

Not that anyone is likely to find such delicacies on this table. About the only 'luxury' food I don't like is truffles, and I'm definitely not a wine buff. Chilean plonk is as good as most people will get, though I used to pick up rare vintages for when Lucian Freud came to lunch, as his palate was as discerning as his palette.

Apart from flowers, almost anything goes as daily table decoration. Fruit, vegetables, objects, even books, are all pressed into use, and they dictate the china I use. I have collections of painted stuff that I like to use at night, whereas in the day I prefer either simple green and white or, more often, a set of scalloped white porcelain that I acquired when my brother John's business unaccountably took over the French manufacturer Giraud. It has the most elaborate, colossal soup tureen, all writhing dolphins on the base, and a lid in the shape of a Rococo shell. It is too vast to use, really, but it makes a dramatic centrepiece.

This porcelain also looks good with the white linen napkins I invariably stick to. Coloured or patterned ones look oddly uninviting to use, and the gleam of white linen in candlelight is so calming. I always light the table with candles in the evening, while low lamps gently illuminate the bird-and-bug painted walls with their soft glow.

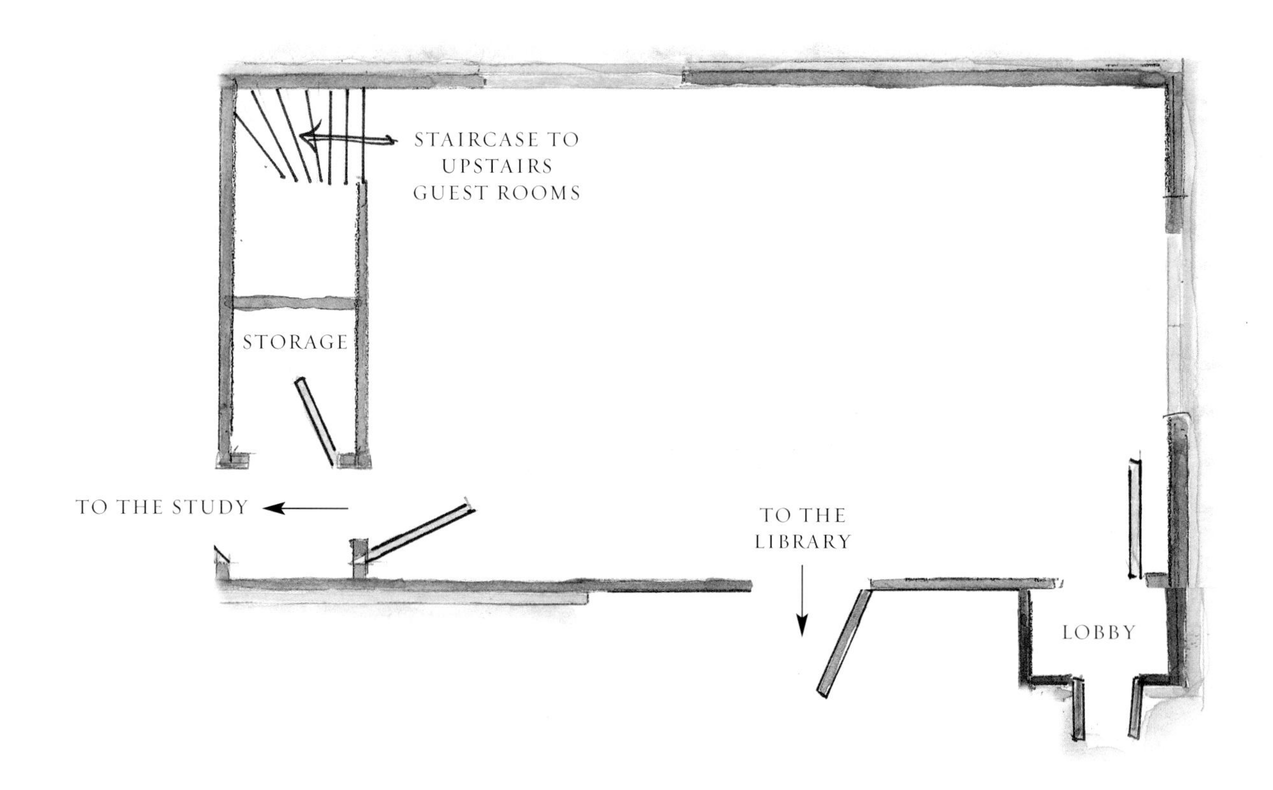

OPPOSITE A fragment of the original wall covering painted on canvas by George Oakes, a master artist, for a house done by John Fowler in London. The concept had been taken by him from a room in Sweden. The owner gave me the 'paper' and I put it up in my London flat.

ABOVE The 'paper' was too fragile to take down and put up successfully yet again, so I had the design copied for this room by Paul Czainski, who, with his wife Chrissie, is the ultimate master of the painted finish. He painted directly onto the walls, but with the wit of making it look like panels by painting in seams, joints and torn edges. There are several pieces of the original in a pretty good state, and one day I will find exactly the spot to use them in.

RIGHT A detail of the painted Gothic borders on the curtains. Their two shades of green complement those in the Chinoiserie 'wallpaper'. The curtains originally hung in the sitting room, where they seemed too overwhelming, so I moved them here.

ABOVE AND TOP RIGHT This Gothic sideboard must once have been a fire surround. Its faux-marble top was painted by my caretaker John Major. Unlike his namesake, he can turn his hand to beautifying anything.

BOTTOM RIGHT The handwriting lamp shades on the shell appliqués were meant to be temporary, but I have grown fond of them.

OPPOSITE The elaborately paned Rococo-style mirror has a kind of thin Fortnum & Mason's 1950s elegance. The pair of brass candle-holding cranes on either side of it call to their big brother painted on the wall below. Paul Czainski's subtle painting of the 'wallpaper' is evident when viewed close up. I especially love the peas in their mauve pod – or a wickedly grinning mouth.

spring lunch

A mere ten minutes' drive away is a superb, award-winning farm shop, Newlyns. Here one can always find the cream of the crop of mainly local – and some imported – fruit, vegetables and, I'm happy to say, Violet Creams. The pears I used for this centrepiece are typical in their luscious perfection, their sealing-wax gleam an eye-catcher amid the whites and greens. The bottle of pink is Britagne, an English rival to Champagne, produced by Coates & Seely at their vineyard nearby. Its taste reminds me of primroses and is eminently suitable for rural rites of spring.

ABOVE LEFT AND OPPOSITE The table seats six perfectly and eight uncomfortably, but who cares? Its surface is a glossy faux marble, the ideal unassuming background for sets of old china. I really only like white napkins, even at gala dinner parties, and I love square-based glassware, like these from William Yeoward.

ABOVE RIGHT Camellias straight from the bush make a luscious and serene table decoration in early spring. Just pick them and plonk them on the table. Here I laid them around a dish of shiny red pears.

COATES & SE

LEFT Green and white hydrangea heads admirably fill out the painted tôle candleholder, making a serene centrepiece. They even look wonderful when they are dried and nearly transparent. The green-curtained door to the right of the window leads to a terrace where I grow herbs in pots.

BELOW A close-up of the spiky dahlia lamp base on the tiled tabletop by the window – about as close as I dare get to it.

festive celebration

There's nothing like gold to gild the lily. So for special occasions I like to lay the table with as much golden glitter as I can find lying around the house. The gilt bronze candlesticks from the console in the old hall are roped in as the foundation on which to build and gild, along with vermeil cutlery. I have a big silver shell that has been allowed to tarnish, so in candlelight it appears golden. I heap it with gold Christmas-tree baubles and scatter more, smaller ones among a mass of gold-encrusted sugared almonds along the centre of the table. A cluster of tealights is buried among them, and their gentle flickering flames reflect in the metal and glassware to create a gala sight.

ABOVE LEFT For festive feasts, either summer birthdays or winter festivities, I like to set the table with golden tones, which glow and glint by candlelight. A silver gilt pitcher from Nicholas Haslam Ltd holds ivy leaves and gold baubles as a centrepiece.

ABOVE RIGHT I use this late Meissen china with the gold look. It's a huge set and so far I haven't broken a single piece – famous last words.

OPPOSITE Large tomatoes filled with caviar soup or lobster cocktail make spectacular impact. I found the vermeil cutlery recently on eBay. Its advantage is that it never needs polishing, unlike silverware.

In the winter, for Christmas or New Year's celebrations, I tend to restrict the colour of the place settings and the first course to green and red for maximum impact when guests gather around the table.

LEFT AND ABOVE Tealights and masses of candles make the golds glimmer. Ivy – straight from the tree – is my favourite Christmas greenery, along with mistletoe.

KITCHEN ETIQUETTE

The small size and lack of width of the kitchen at the Hunting Lodge preclude the lovely, squashy dog-height sofa and vast telly, or huge round table loaded with home-baked delights fresh from the Aga, which I so envy at friends' houses.

The best way to treat my compact kitchen was for it to be utilitarian with some attractive embellishments. As little more than a passage from old house to 'new', it has to be pretty functional, and, I hope, functionally pretty. The main thing is to be able to quickly hide the detritus of cooking from the eyes of people walking through it to the dining room. There is no sadder sight than greasy pans and slops. I've solved this by having chopping boards big enough to cover both sinks – though, of course, one can bung a lot of the mess into the larder until later.

But the great thing about the kitchen's size is that everything is within easy reach, and the high shelf running all round the room can adequately house the more boring-looking pots and pans. The plain deal table gets pulled out whenever kitchen supper is on the menu. With a tablecloth

RIGHT The kitchen is literally the centre of the house. You have to go through it to get from one part of the house to the other, hence, it can't be too gussied up. The oak table pulls out to eat kitchen suppers at, and everything one needs is within hand's reach.

The Cookery Year

ABOVE LEFT A row of prettily painted doors hide essentials, such as plates, table linen and glassware, in the pantry between the kitchen and the old hall. Opposite them is a wide counter, with more cupboards underneath, providing a convenient dumping ground for the mass of stuff I seem to bring down from London most weekends.

LEFT Warhol's *Queen*, Brian Ferry and Colette van den Thillart, NH Design's creative director, are permanently wedged in the frame of an old map of Buckinghamshire, which actually marks Great Hundridge Manor, the house where I was born.

OPPOSITE Great Hundridge Manor is shown in the watercolour by John Hookham, which hangs above the butcher's block. I like red stripes and checks in the kitchen, as opposed to the usual blues or greens.

over it and a couple of candles lit, and the red-striped 'dishcloth'-material curtains pulled, the little room looks surprisingly cosy and inviting.

Luckily, there is a pantry nearby with a bank of all-concealing cupboards behind painted panelled doors. This is where the better china and glassware are kept, and opposite, in green baize-lined drawers, the cutlery.

A snag is that the kitchen is the only place in the house where the Internet works perfectly, so there's often a queue of friends grumpily hugging their laptops.

LEFT This is the view from the flower room, which links the kitchen with the library, through the internal window to the lobby and back door beyond.

OPPOSITE Baskets collected over the years hang on the walls in the little space between the back door and the flower room – so called because it's where I keep many of my vases and containers, and thus where I often arrange the flowers for the house. The two flat fish-shaped baskets were used for grape harvesting on Monte Argentario in southern Tuscany.

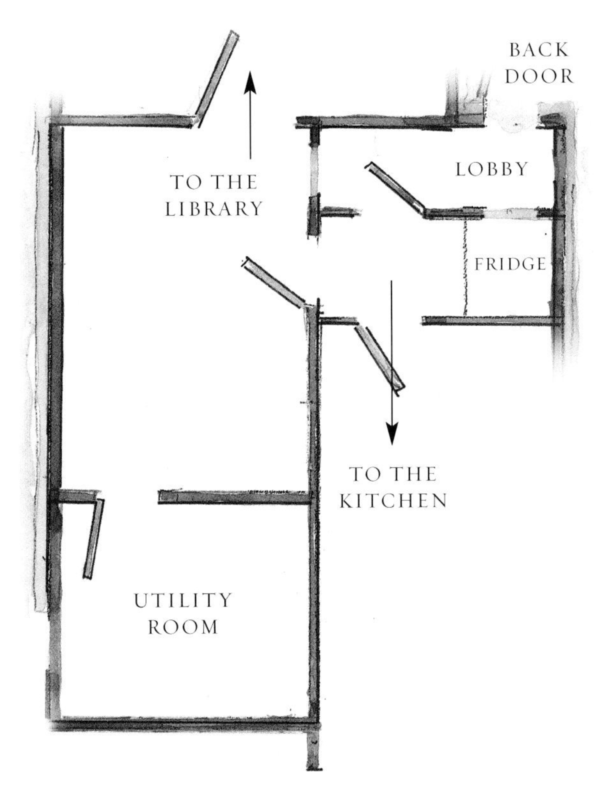

THE FLOWER ROOM

Books have invaded this room as well, but there is still a bit of wall space left on which to hang the odd-shaped and sized baskets I pick up on my travels. They also dangle from hooks in the rafters above. The shelves (see page 156) hold a motley crew of vases and containers. Among my favourites is the three-tiered one on the lowest shelf, which has a row of test tubes in each tier. Anything looks good in it, and children love to fill it with the daises and buttercups clutched in their tight little fists after a country ramble. The jug, apparently made of twisted rope, I found recently when participating in the annual Rochester Sweeps Festival, and the pineapple-shaped one doubles up for juice at breakfast. Below them are a couple in Italian earthenware. They were my father's when he lived in Rome in the early 1900s, so must have some age and, I hope, value.

LEFT Above the painted Victorian table, flower vases and other containers sit on the *only* shelves without books in the house. My portrait on the wall in the red library beyond was painted for me by Vanessa Garwood.

BELOW A rather unstable Lutyens-style chair is not meant to be sat on. Behind it hangs an early design for the ceiling of a shell grotto.

BEDTIME
STORIES

The three bedrooms upstairs are all no bigger than the rooms below, but mine, its three windows giving onto the lawn and surrounding forest, with the lake glinting in the distance, seems more spacious than it is.

The room is suffused with pearly light glancing on the soft grey-blue walls. White accentuates this tranquil, lambent atmosphere, particularly the sheets and pillows picked out with pale blue detailing, specially designed for me by that doyenne of bed linens, Gayle Warwick. Above is a corona with a canopy of nineteenth-century French glazed chintz, which emphasizes in colour and line the vertically placed strips of wallpaper border. Both the canopy and the barely patterned curtains have narrow edgings of crimson cotton to give them definition.

RIGHT Evening light filters through the lattice-pane windows, deepening the shadows in my bedroom and dressing room to a radiant blue. The Gothic chairs were also in my house in Waterloo.

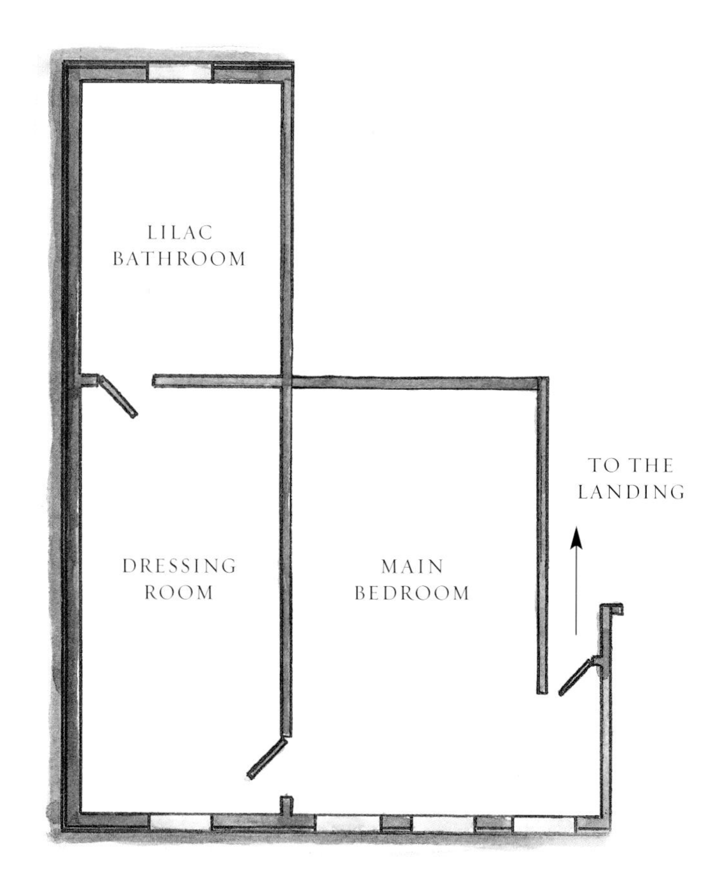

ABOVE My bedroom is directly above the sitting room with which it shares a chimney flue. Above the fireplace is a Regency gilded bamboo looking glass that was in my mother's bedroom at Hundridge. The pictures are all haphazardly collected, though the general theme is one of children playing games, as depicted in these engravings on the mantelshelf. The doll was given to me by Eugenia Mikulina, the delightful editor of Russian *Architectural Digest*, and I found the blackened icon in a street market in St Petersburg; it was probably painted yesterday, but who cares?

OPPOSITE A ruffled chintz shade on an Etruscan-style porcelain lamp – also my mother's – continues the floral theme of the wallpaper borders and, along with the roses and urn, echoes the colours of the fabrics used in the room. There is usually a tiny television on the buff-painted Victorian chest of drawers.

LA TROTTOLA

The simplicity of the fabrics creates the airy, restful atmosphere that I believe all bedrooms should impart.

LEFT A 1930s bogus 'Chinoiserie' chiffonier catches the eye at the doorway to the dressing room. Atop is a pile of hats and a carved wooden finial that I've often copied in plaster. The grey and blue painted early Victorian Gothic chair is one of a pair.

ABOVE This lamp is one of three brought back from Mexico by my father in the 1920s. It is a bottle clad in leather, forming an effigy of a peasant woman.

OPPOSITE Boots and more boots fit snugly under the chest and bamboo-trimmed table. The mirror reflects the white 'marbleizing' I had painted to disguise the plastered-over cracks.

The adjacent dressing room continues the blue and buff colour scheme, though here, architectural drawings and plans line the walls. The green label tied to the tall chest belonged to Simon Fleet, who, with his house 'The Gothic Box' in South Kensington, was my first aesthetic inspiration when I left school. Simon also gave me the tile with 'NicKy liVeS hEre' written on it, which sits on top of the loo in my bathroom; it's been in every house I've ever lived in. On the wall beside it are old engravings of mermaids and mermen, so naturalistic it makes one think they must have existed.

b

OPPOSITE The curtains in my bathroom were here in John Fowler's day. If you look carefully, you will see that the flower design is upside down on the left-hand one, so he must have had only this length of stuff left over from a job. The carpet, made especially for me, is a kind of blurred moss and extremely good at not showing stains.

ABOVE These manganese-coloured tiles, which I had manufactured in St Petersburg, line the shower.

RIGHT This carriage lamp is one of a pair that sit on the wall on either side of the washbasin. They must have come from a film set because they are made of some weird rubbery substance.

That most chic of American ladies, New York socialite Nan Kempner, always said, 'Give a woman a pink bathroom and she's happy.' But mine, a more masculine shade of blue-lilac grey, seems to do the trick, and feels like an extension of the dressing room next door.

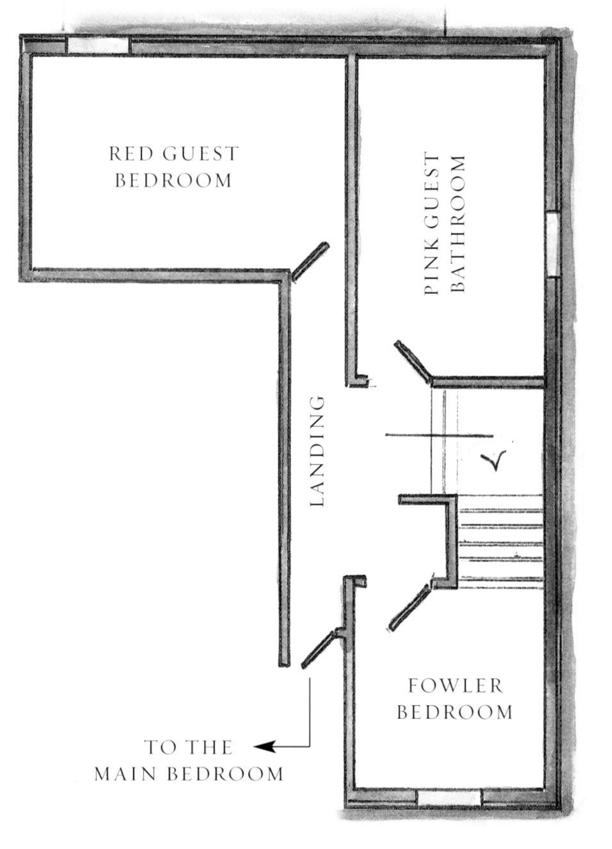

FOR GUESTS

A couple of guests can be vaguely comfortable in these bedrooms, provided they aren't total strangers. They can sleep in the striped room, with Gayle Warwick's red-embroidered sheets and pillows, and use the Fowler bedroom and its pagoda wardrobe as an overflow for clothes and suitcases. At least they have a bathroom to themselves. But when there are three staying in this part of the house, the comfort zone gets a bit hugger-mugger and I shut my

OPPOSITE, LEFT The new striped bedroom is exactly that. Stripes of any width in the same colour seem to work, especially if there is something solid, in this case the curtains, to unify them. The bedside lamps are painted Baroque altar candlesticks. I'm not mad about using churchy things, but these are secular enough to be light-hearted.

OPPOSITE, RIGHT All the accessories have been chosen to tie in with the colour scheme. Splashes of red are introduced on the coat of the beggar in the framed poster by Lovat Fraser and in the uniforms of the soldier silhouettes on each side of it. One is actually painted, but the other, on the right, is a nearly identical postcard.

ABOVE The eagle glowering from his rocky perch came as part of a job lot in a saleroom buy and cried out for something flowing beneath him. Luckily, I had this length of narrow striped red cotton to make a swag from – just the ticket. Gayle Warwick made the bed linen with its fine red stitching to complete the picture.

OPPOSITE The pink guest bathroom is carpeted with the same stuff as my own bathroom. After I had the NH Design table painted with random spots, the Gothic chair cried out for a little amateur touch-up in pink, by me.

ABOVE The bathroom walls are covered with Bartolozzi and Angelica Kauffman sepia rondels – though, in fact, the top one on the left is a watercolour by French illustrator and author Philippe Jullian.

The colour of the guest bathroom is very flattering. The window lets in lots of light, and the furniture and pictures jolly it up no end.

eyes to their obvious distress, and just pray the immersion heater holds out. Personally, as a guest, I don't mind a small bedroom as long as the bathroom is a decent size, and surprisingly the pink guest bathroom is quite spacious.

In the newer part of the house, above the dining room, are two more bedrooms and a bathroom, offering plenty of space for accommodating weekend guests.

THE FOWLER BEDROOM

John Fowler seems to have had the same feeling about small bedrooms as I do, as the one he chose to use is almost monk-like in its dimensions. In the 1960s, at my ranch in Arizona, I had the smallest bed imaginable; narrow and tall with four posts, it had been made by an itinerant carpenter, who appeared out of the desert one day. That room was cool blue and white, but here the warm, mellow buttery walls and black and lemon-yellow accents banish any notion of constriction. The room is soothing and serene, and even the most insomnolent of guests tell me they are lulled to sleep by the gentle breezes rustling through the magnolia leaves that frame the arched, diamond-paned window.

ABOVE John Fowler slept in this minuscule room when he lived here – hence the bells to summon household staff beside the narrow bed. The ribboned bedhead goes well with the black-framed apes and animals on the wall alongside it. They were my father's; he had a thing about monkeys.

OPPOSITE We practically had to take the house apart to get this octagonal cloth-covered clothes case into the room. It was far bigger than it looked when I bought it at an antiques fair.

LEFT Looking into the tiny bedroom from the hall, with its extravagant Mauny wallpaper, the warm buttery cream of the walls and curtains provides a delightfully simple contrast.

ABOVE The carpet in the Fowler bedroom is the same as in both of the bathrooms – in strong light it almost looks white. The pattern on the bed valance chimes well with it. As the great decorator Nancy Lancaster insisted, 'To make a room look quiet, you have to complicate everything.'

OPPOSITE Amateur paintings hang above an Edwardian black-lacquer chest of drawers. The one bang above it, of the Hunting Lodge by moonlight, I found in a junk shop in Putney. Min Hogg gave me the watercolour to the right, which is by our friend Barbara Dorf, when I first got the house. The one above is by Bruce Hollingsworth, whom I remember having a decorating business in the 1950s. Opposite is a very early watercolour by me of the Malcontenta outside Venice.

THE PERFECT
SETTING

COME OUTSIDE

The garden, reclaimed after decades of neglect, was laid out by John Fowler in the early 1950s. The sitting room opens onto the terrace, with its views across the rectangular lawn bordered by square-cut hornbeam trees, which leads through a gate to the meadow and lake beyond.

The terrace in front of the house, laid with old, found bricks echoing those towering above, runs the whole width of the façade. Four squares, their centres in-filled with dark-grey smooth pebbles, are its only decoration and form bases for the Versailles boxes containing topiary. This simple apron makes an even(ish) base that is wide enough for several pieces of grey-painted iron outdoor furniture. Yet, from a distance, the terrace is subtly invisible, so the house appears to rise seamlessly from the chequerboard-mown lawn.

I try to leave the furniture out as long as the weather permits, even if it does mean a yearly slosh of paint, for the terrace is as important as an extra room. I like to have drinks there whenever possible and often dine outside when it's warm enough. Even on quite nippy days we tend to gather there, with the fire's warmth spilling comfortingly out through the open door. The metal-fringed table and the chairs and benches are a variation of styles, which is much prettier and more relaxed than if they were all matching.

OPPOSITE The Hunting Lodge seen from across the lake. I mow the ride from the garden gate down through the meadow, where we have viciously fought the bracken so that now, in spring and summer, it is a sea of wild flowers, including masses of rare bee orchids.

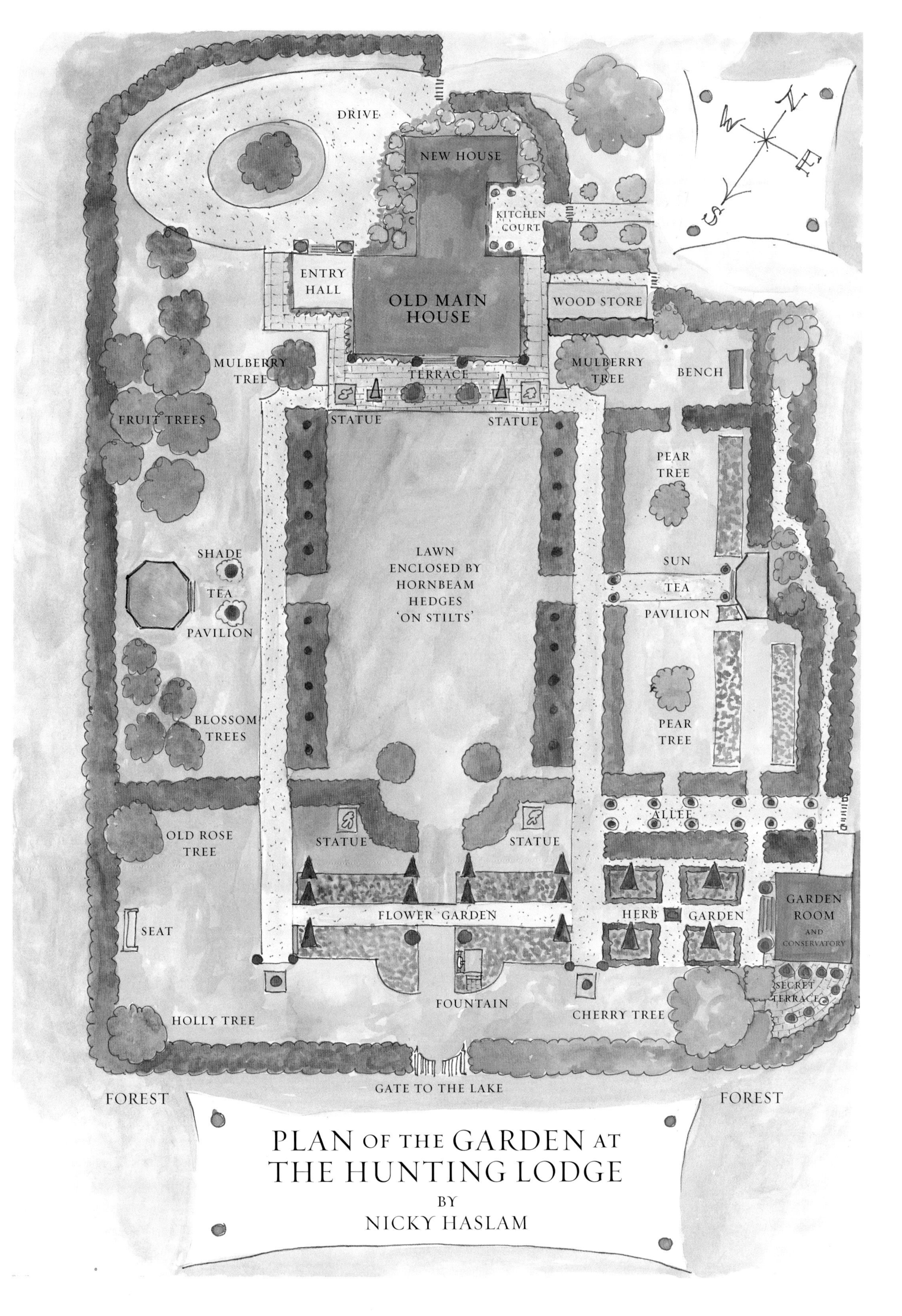
DRIVE
NEW HOUSE
KITCHEN COURT
ENTRY HALL
OLD MAIN HOUSE
WOOD STORE
MULBERRY TREE
TERRACE
MULBERRY TREE
BENCH
STATUE
STATUE
FRUIT TREES
PEAR TREE
LAWN ENCLOSED BY HORNBEAM HEDGES 'ON STILTS'
SHADE
TEA
PAVILION
SUN
TEA
PAVILION
PEAR TREE
BLOSSOM TREES
ALLEE
OLD ROSE TREE
STATUE
STATUE
FLOWER GARDEN
HERB GARDEN
GARDEN ROOM AND CONSERVATORY
SEAT
SECRET TERRACE
FOUNTAIN
HOLLY TREE
CHERRY TREE
GATE TO THE LAKE
FOREST
FOREST
PLAN OF THE GARDEN AT THE HUNTING LODGE
BY
NICKY HASLAM

PREVIOUS PAGES A rectangular lawn, as wide as the house itself, lies in front of the façade. It is shorn crossways alternately at each mowing to give a chequerboard effect. One of my first tasks on taking on this beautiful but somewhat overgrown marvel was to draw a bird's-eye plan of it, roughly to scale. This was so that I could envisage the area as a whole and fathom what led to what, as Fowler's layout, inspired by those he had admired in eighteenth-century Dutch pictures and engravings, was a series of 'connecting' but part-hidden rooms.

ABOVE AND OPPOSITE Early morning sun after a frost picks out the brick moulding around the windows and doors with limelight clarity. At the end of the terrace, Spring, puffing on a clay pipe with his dog at his heels, gazes though mulberry boughs at the distant lake.

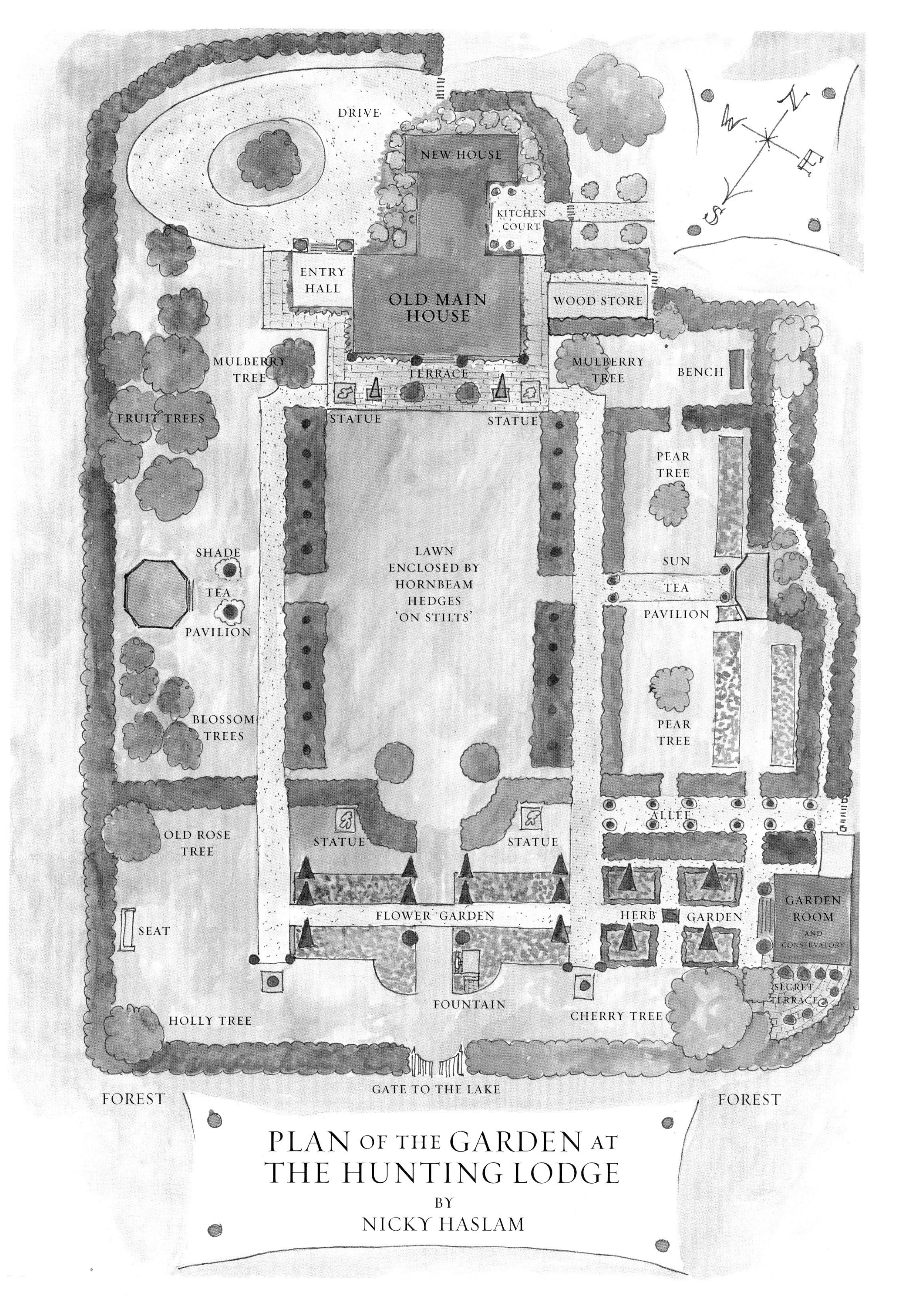

PLAN OF THE GARDEN AT
THE HUNTING LODGE
BY
NICKY HASLAM

PREVIOUS PAGES A rectangular lawn, as wide as the house itself, lies in front of the façade. It is shorn crossways alternately at each mowing to give a chequerboard effect. One of my first tasks on taking on this beautiful but somewhat overgrown marvel was to draw a bird's-eye plan of it, roughly to scale. This was so that I could envisage the area as a whole and fathom what led to what, as Fowler's layout, inspired by those he had admired in eighteenth-century Dutch pictures and engravings, was a series of 'connecting' but part-hidden rooms.

ABOVE AND OPPOSITE Early morning sun after a frost picks out the brick moulding around the windows and doors with limelight clarity. At the end of the terrace, Spring, puffing on a clay pipe with his dog at his heels, gazes though mulberry boughs at the distant lake.

The pair of Gothic benches and some chairs have matching squabs of 'Melba', one of the first fabrics I ever designed, and fortuitously splashed with pinkish magnolia boughs on green stripes, echoing the magnolia tree against the wall – not that it ever flowers. Can anyone help? The chairs around the dining table are cushioned in simple green-and-white stripes in the classic Elsie Mendl tradition, but I sometimes yearn to redo the whole lot in scarlet-hollyhock-flowered black chintz, something I saw at Belvoir Castle in my youth, and which has remained with me as being incredibly chic. Too chic, perhaps, for this rather humbler setting.

OPPOSITE The terrace in early summer, before the box, Portugal laurels and hornbeam hedges have had the first of their two, sometimes three, annual haircuts.

BELOW Seen from the garden door, which opens from the sitting room on to the terrace, hornbeam screens at the end of the lawn hide the colour-filled flowerbeds beyond them, creating a *tapis vert*.

RIGHT The non-intrusive mix of pale brick and 'stone' wood blockwork is apparent behind Summer, preparing herself for the long, languid days ahead.

While I can't pretend to be a plantsman, though I'm getting better with trial and error, I can, and have, 'designed' gardens, and they are usually loosely based on the one here at the Hunting Lodge.

terrace supper

I can always think up no end of reasons to have supper outside, even if that means being bundled up in rugs and Barbours. Of course, the main excuse is that there is nothing more enchanting than candlelight outdoors, not only on the table, but also in lanterns hung from sturdy branches and in the sconces, which throw golden halos against the russet masonry. The cliché that food tastes better outside is even truer with flickering flames.

Sometimes, with luck, one can stay here until the candles gutter and the stars gleam recognizably above. Once in a blue one, the moon, when full, casts a ghostly pallor on to the lawn, and the high hornbeam hedges become inky walls, shutting out even the surrounding forest. Then one can imagine that this chiaroscuro stage will gradually become alive with the spectral singers of some forgotten fugue, the lonely piping of a statue of a Pan-like shepherd, a ballet danced by transfigured swans, as owls blink and hoot in the velvet curtain of leaves.

THIS PAGE Nothing is more romantic than candles outdoors on a rare breathless dusk, and I found an old French iron candle-cage to hang from the magnolia branch above the dining table. The ever-possible risk of a gust of wind plunging us into darkness can be solved by those incredible battery-operated candles that look equally magical, though on a still evening one can't beat the real thing. I like to line the *sous-plats* with mulberry or vine leaves, and use a set of Victorian green and white china on them.

The surrounding woods are among the oldest in England. The lane to the house winds through groves of oaks, many of which were reputedly planted soon after the Norman Conquest.

OPPOSITE, TOP A garden for all seasons. A light frost dusts the grass in winter, silhouetting the bare shapes of the planting. The geometric box plants form a dramatic glossy green counterpoint to the soft browns and russets of the foliage-free trees.

OPPOSITE, BOTTOM LEFT AND RIGHT The old pump's water supply comes from a natural reservoir deep below the lawn. Its crank handle was the only means by which former inhabitants could get water for their daily needs.

RIGHT For years I felt the pump needed a friend in the corresponding right-hand bed, so last spring I asked my caretaker John Major to construct this trelliswork twin. By summer it was already bursting with scented jasmine and honeysuckle.

OVERLEAF The lace-like branches of hornbeams 'on stilts' are gilded by the winter sun. The view from this angle always reminds me of photographs by Eugène Atget, a French, turn-of-the-last-century genius with a camera, and his evocative series of the gardens at Versailles – on a less profligate scale, I should add.

This is the ideal small garden, laid out originally by John Fowler, the planting planned by his cousin Bunty Oakley. They created this grandeur on a small scale, with the largest 'rooms' having green walls of trees pierced with tall vistas through to trellised pavilions, and a *clairvoie* though the opened gates to the meadow sweeping down to a glistening sheet of water. Hidden from this *salon vert* are banks of flowers, an old pump gushing into a stone basin and, almost out of sight, the garden room.

OPPOSITE A golden hop quickly smothers this pavilion in early summer. Some summers, I leave it to grow rampantly at will; others, I cut it strenuously back. Either way, it's that blessed spot, a suntrap; even in winter's grip, slanting rays illumine its glowing interior, a magnet for a break with a steaming cup of broth while marvelling at frost-laced branches, still, against the sky.

ABOVE AND RIGHT Both pavilions, which face each other across the lawn, are enticing places to pause or rest in every season. We often have after-dinner coffee in either, though this one has the added beauty of the breeze-rustled forest leaves behind its open-trellised windows. The carved-wood bunch of grapes hanging over the table is an early shop sign.

ABOVE RIGHT George Oakes originally painted the phantom oak trees onto the melon-coloured walls (see also overleaf). With a little judicious touching up from time to time, they have remained as palely perfect as the day they were done.

THIS PAGE AND OPPOSITE The pavilion on the left side of the lawn gets sun almost all day, so it's the perfect place to lay out a hearty snack of bread smothered with butter and chunks of cheese and ham. George Oakes's peaceful treescapes, painted in grisaille on the rough yellow plaster, add a touch of sylvan tranquillity.

gardeners' lunch

The straightening of backs relieved from weeding, the clang of tools being stacked, the crunch of hobnailed boots on gravel signifying a break for doorstep sandwiches and a mug of hot, sweet tea always remind me of old Gibbs, the gardener at Hundridge. It is a tradition I maintain, as here in the painted pavilion my gardeners, Martin and Gerald, discuss garden strategy. I say discuss, but it's really one-sided, as they know what will actually work, unlike my airy-fairy schemes. When to plant, when to trim and when to prune are their fortes, and pooh-poohing my unsuitable suggestions their politeness. So I leave them to it, meekly reminding them that on the whole, I only like pink flowers, with white near the house and perhaps a splash of crimson in the borders. But they subtly weave in blues and yellows, so of course in spring, when these hues first burst into bloom, one's spirit soars. And in the autumn, when tawny gold mingled with smudgy, claret-coloured planting echoes the crab apples, damsons and oaks swaying, laden, above, I am annually, perennially, eternally grateful.

The subtlety of this layout is that only green of different intensities can be seen until the eye roves beyond and finds other 'rooms' – some of box, some beech, filled with flowers and dotted with statuary, urns, trelliswork, pavilions and clematis-clambered pear-tree arches.

OPPOSITE AND THIS PAGE I like the fact that informal English gardens have a natural progression, colour-wise, from all shades of blue in spring, then to white. Early summer brings a profusion of pinks in the form of moss roses and peonies, and later pale and deep reds. If I am being honest, I don't really like yellow or orange flowers, so that colour palette suits me fine. I also like to add in wild flowers, particularly ox-eye daisies and ragged robin, and often transplant them from the central reservation of a nearby road, before the council machine comes along and churns them into oblivion. Wild foxglove and geranium seeds get scattered willy-nilly over the beds, adding height and colour, though one has to be watchful for those ever-invasive poppies.

THE CONSERVATORY

Conservatories, nowadays, tend to end up as second living rooms, with vast scraggy sofas, the old telly pushed into re-service once the flat screen arrives, and piles of dog-eared mags. No such luck, in my case. The wirework table, some iron garden chairs, plus a couple in extruded fibreglass – very 1950s – have to suffice as creature comforts for impromptu meals under the fructiferous vine that twists and turns across the glazed (and somewhat leaky, I notice) roof.

Apart from a tall Baroque-shaped, green-painted 'Dutch' cupboard, which holds the Turkish-inspired plates given to me by OKA supremo Annabel Astor, all the walls are taken up by working-height slatted shelves holding a host of pots with geraniums and petunias, which somehow manage to defy my signal lack in the green finger department. Under these are the bigger pots waiting for summer occupants, log containers for the garden room's recently installed fire, tools, twine and baskets. The best, most practical bit of the room is the floor – squares of duckboard, laid in crisscross fashion direct on the concrete and a doddle to lift up for an occasional hose-down.

RIGHT Planting out being prepared in early summer: white petunias are the only bearable ones. The wrought-iron chairs conveniently fold up to make more space for the attendant messiness that the process always seems to involve. The open doorway on the left leads into the garden room.

Nobody could say much is actually conserved in here, but it has a delightful nonchalance all year round – all green-dappled glass and grapes in summer and that nostalgic scent of damp soil and sleeping nature in winter.

OPPOSITE I pick up fallen branches in the woods to fill the essential log basket. They dry out quickly in the warmth of the sun, ready for the greedy fire in the garden room. The painted Gothic standing shelves house twine and plant labels in old baskets.

ABOVE LEFT These rustic steps are a boon when reaching for the highest-growing clusters of delectably sweet grapes. The floor is squares of duckboard from B&Q, easy to lift when hosing off the concrete beneath.

ABOVE RIGHT I tend to stick to geraniums, as they do so well and are easily transportable in their Victorian flowerpots to needy places in the main house.

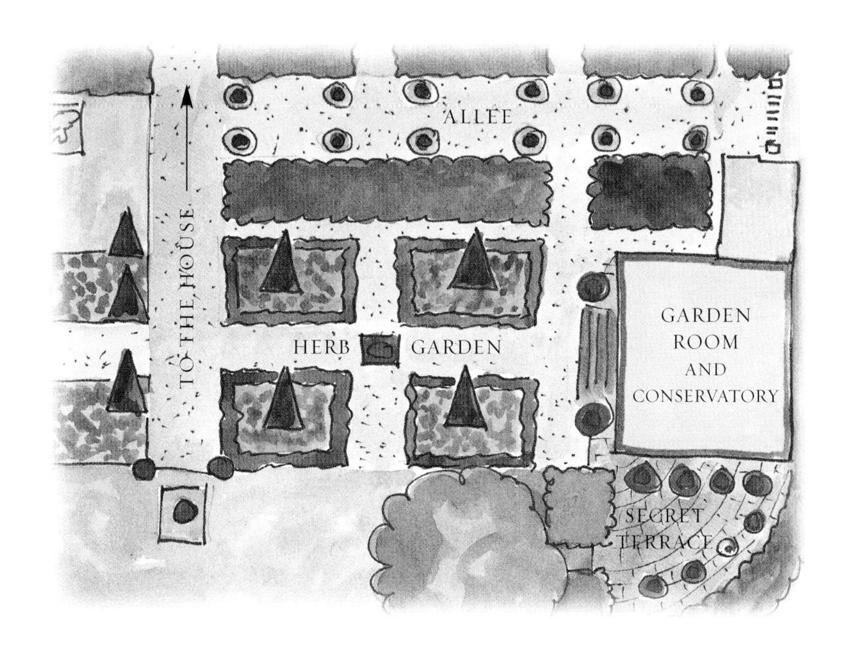

Food tastes better in the open air, and even more so in a vine-garlanded setting such as this, without the bother of rugs and hampers, no ants, and no furious batting away at wasps.

conservatory lunch

Eating down in the conservatory is always rather a random affair, more of an indoor picnic. As often happens, the skies will clear mid-morning – the old adage 'rain before seven, shine before eleven' usually holds strangely true. Then all thoughts of dining-room lunch flee, and it's all hands on deck to whip up a tempting spread. Fish, smothered in fennel, to grill on the makeshift barbeque; eggs mayonnaise with anchovies (canned, of course – fresh ones are pointless); tomatoes with sweet red onions and pomegranate; garden-gathered greens for a salad (did you know ground-elder, that bane of gardeners' lives, was introduced to England by the Elizabethans as a spinach-like vegetable, and jolly good it is) to go with a wheel of Wigmore, the superb local sheep's-milk cheese and far superior to commonplace Brie. Add to that a stack of various breads (spelt flour for me) and slabs of salty butter, and Bob's your uncle. And then to follow, in spring, a dish of cherries; in summer, grapes by the bunch, hanging above; and, in the autumn, plums and blackberries, if you can be fished to forage. Wash it down with a Hampshire vineyard white wine or a slug of homemade damson gin, and a good, long kip on the lawn or by the fire is guaranteed.

THIS PAGE AND OPPOSITE A South-of-France-style lunch set out on the wirework table is very informal, given the nature of the room. The painted 'Dutch' cupboard holds the wherewithal for easy eating, and the baskets hanging from hooks overhead double up as serving dishes.

OLIVE

THE GARDEN ROOM

I rather wish I had dreamt up a more romantic name – the summer pavilion, or something – for this all-important building, rather than the somewhat obvious garden room. But that's exactly what it is, and with other pavilions dotted about the place, the simplicity avoids confusion.

I say all-important, as it is the only room here that can hold more than about six people with any ease, and it is delightfully enticing to use all year round ever since I installed the fireplace. Even in winter we can scurry down the lawn to settle in the two new hearthside sofas and put some opera, good and loud, on the hi-fi. A small hob and fridge hidden in the wallpapered entry lobby save having to go up to the kitchen for necessities for entertaining.

In warm weather, with the door and French windows wide open, the *trio vistas* through the conservatory, the garden room and the garden beyond create a cool and colourful enfilade. With nicotiana, lilies, rosemary and mint scenting the evening air, one can flop onto one of the four Gothic octagonal seats in the box garden for a long, cooling drink.

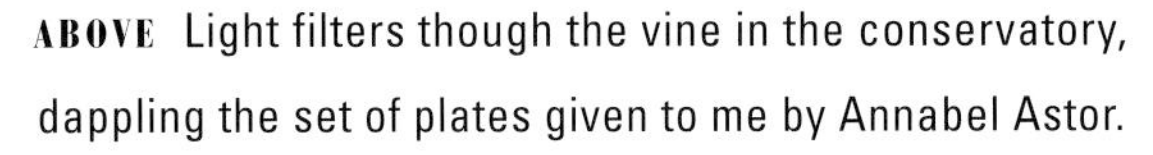

ABOVE Light filters though the vine in the conservatory, dappling the set of plates given to me by Annabel Astor.

ABOVE RIGHT By the conservatory door is a mahogany cupboard, once a pull-down bed (surely from the dressing room of some irritated husband), which I've converted into a many-shelved hiding place for CDs, hi-fi gubbins and glasses. Atop is a tin agave plant in a stone urn.

OPPOSITE The same fabric as on the sofas is glued to the rather brutal back legs of this table – the other half of the console in the dining room – to make them easier on the eye. John Fowler's tassel-branched lantern hangs serenely above. I once copied it at about eight times the size for a commission in Moscow.

LEFT I put in the fireplace the room always lacked; the English Rococo surround was found at an antiques fair. The sepia-grisaille portrait over it is of James Thompson, author of the words to 'Rule, Britannia!'. Each side of it hang oils by Michael Wishart, the British artist with whom I lived at his house on a hilltop above St Tropez in the late 1950s, before that earthly paradise began its slide into inexorable vulgarity. Beyond is his watercolour of my head as a bouquet of roses. John Major transformed the pineapple ice pail from sludgy orange to fresh green and white.

ABOVE When the box parterre is at its lushest in scent and colour, I like to sit there and breathe it all in. I could never find seats neat enough to fit in the four corners until I saw these quatrefoil-stamped resin planters in the local garden centre. Upturned, painted and squab-cushioned, they make the perfect perch for an early-evening drink.

LEFT 'Ye spotted snakes with double tongue' comes to mind when seeing this appliqué with its chintz half-shade.

OPPOSITE These French windows open on to a small brick-paved terrace surrounded by a high yew hedge, its top clipped into crenellated battlements. It's the best possible place for sunbathing – dry and sheltered and, most importantly, not overlooked. Within the room, touches of scarlet enliven the many muted shades of carpet, canework and chintz. On the sofa is a frilled cushion in the carnation print that covered both sofas before I quite recently redecorated the room.

OVERLEAF, LEFT One of a couple of Swedish-style chairs sits in a corner near the French window that gives on to the paved terrace. The other French window opens on to the box parterre. The curtain material is 'Balcony Stripe' in cream on white linen, from my latest collection, 'Random Harvest'. The plates on the bookshelves, unearthed in a car-boot sale for £4, are post-war pottery, and their typical Festival of Britain border design is refreshingly geometric amid all the patterns elsewhere.

OVERLEAF, RIGHT I've had the startlingly pink cloisonné lamp since I spotted it in New York in the 1960s. The rough wood writing desk on which it stands is, in fact, an old shop serving counter, complete with slot for the odd *sous*; I saw it forlornly abandoned in the back alleys of Bordeaux. The picture hanging above is by Henry Hudson, from his *Rake's Progress* series; it is made from Plasticine and spilled wine. The landscape oils are by Robin Day (left) and Tory Oaksey (right).

Light is what makes the room. The three French windows facing south and west allow maximum sunlight almost all day, but, filtered through near-transparent curtains, it is muted and soft. This takes any strident tones out of the chintz-covered furniture, harmonizes the faded colours in the carpet and gives the plain painted walls their pale biscuit-brown glow. The walls are anchored by faux-marble paintwork on the skirting boards and door frames, its coffee-and-cream striations merging quietly into the scrubbed pine floorboards. This relatively neutral shell 'contains' the room, and allows its contents to speak for themselves. Friends often come here to write and read in total peace; there is no phone or television to disturb or tempt – just firelight, opera, a drinks tray and, on frosty mornings, that light casting a silver sheen in this most gently talkative of rooms.

CYRIL CONNOLLY
GARNET PUDDING
Barbara Pym
VITA
WINNER TAKES ALL
FAMILY SECRETS
NATHANIEL'S NUTMEG
TO THE POINT
TONY BLAIR

OPPOSITE A pool of light glimmers on the unruffled water. The lake is fed by a small stream from a spring high up in the downs, which goes under the nearby canal and somehow magically bubbles up the other side.

ABOVE The lake and stream have a rather primeval atmosphere in winter; as dusk falls, one longs to hurry home to toast and toddy.

OVERLEAF Weak winter light gilds the water-lilies under the weeping willow on the island, its rays reflecting on the lake's calm surface. In a few weeks a swan and his pen will arrive to start a new family of cygnets. And I will watch them, reflecting on my luck of living in this sublime folly as a new year unfolds.

THE LAKE

As I write, the evening sun is sending searchlight-sharp shafts through wind-swayed trees. And in this radiance I see the swans, which come each spring to the little island in the lake, have winged in for an impromptu visit. There's the cob, twisting his long, lithe, snowy neck among the bulrushes, and his pen, fussing about with her tail feathers. The breathtaking thing is that they are with their five cygnets, hatched here in April, and almost fully grown, now nearly all-white, their beaks not yet onyx dark. Rarely does the entire brood survive; mink and other monsters defeat their mother's constant marshalling as they whizz, cheeping, over the cloud-reflected surface. But this year all have survived nature's perils; perhaps this rare visit is to show them their birthplace? Maybe these children will, in turn, come to breed here, to fill one's heart with thumping joy when, after winter's rain and ruin, those immaculate, phantom-like forms descend with a showy silver splash as the primroses fade.

Somehow, the duck population has almost tripled this last summer. God knows, they had the weather for it. Fairly tame, they clamber out on those ridiculous feet to gobble the provender thrown for them, only to waddle away, squawking angrily, at a sudden movement.

This low-lying land is called, unappealingly, Lousy Moor, derived from *low-sea mere*. Such ancient language connections make my spine tingle. As does the connection to so long ago, every time I see the obelisk on the lake's far bank, part-hidden by the willows on the water. It is merely painted hardboard, but its fading inscription honours an extraordinary woman, Lady Juliet Duff, already a legend in my youth, both on her own account and for her mother, Lady Ripon, who persuaded Diaghilev to bring his *Ballets Russes* to London. This ephemeral memorial stood in the garden of Lady Juliet's house in Wilton and was given to me, when she died, by Lord Pembroke. I envy her constant gaze across the limpid, tree-circled water, and on, up the wild orchid-dotted meadow, to the enchanting rose-hued façade of the Hunting Lodge.

NICKY'S FAVOURITE SOURCES

ARCHITECTS

IKE, KLIGERMAN, BARKLEY
440 West 42nd St, (ste 11)
New York, NY 10036, USA
+1 (0)917 570 2002
www.ikba.com

TIMOTHY HATTON ARCHITECTS
Canal Floor, The RB Building,
Portobello Dock, 557 Harrow
Road, London W10 4RH
+44 (0)20 3235 0070
www.thal.co.uk

MUNKENBECK + PARTNERS
135 Curtain Road,
London EC2A 3BX
+44 (0)20 7739 3300
www.mandp.uk.com

CONSTRUCTION

CHELSEA CONSTRUCTION
1 Port House, Plantation
Wharf, London SW11 3TY
+44 (0)20 7350 0990
www.chelsea-construction.co.uk

WALLPAPER

ALTFIELD
Design Centre Chelsea
Harbour, London SW10 0XE
+44 (0)20 7351 5893
www.altfield.com

FROMENTAL
Saga Centre, 326 Kensal Road,
London W10 5BX
+44 (0)20 3410 2000
www.fromental.co.uk

GEORGE SPENCER DESIGNS
33 Elystan Street,
London SW3 3NT
+44 (0)20 7584 3003
www.georgespencer.com

TATIANA TAFUR LTD
672 King's Road,
London SW6 2DY
+44 (0)20 7731 3777
www.tatianatafur.com

TONES SPECIALIST
PAPERHANGERS LTD
3 Stocks Lane, Gamlingay,
Sandy, Bedfordshire SG19 3JP
+44 (0)1767 650277
www.specialistpaperhangers.co.uk

ZUBER
3 Rue des Saints Péres,
75006 Paris, France
+33 (0)142 779 591
42 Pimlico Road, London
SW1W 8LP
+44 (0)20 7824 8265
www.zuber.fr

PAINT

FARROW AND BALL
Uddens Estate, Wimborne,
Dorset BH21 7NL
+44 (0)1202 876141
www.farrow-ball.com

LITTLE GREENE
Wood Street, Manchester
M11 2FB
+44 (0)845 880 5855
www.littlegreene.com

PAINT & PAPER LIBRARY
David Oliver Limited, 5 Elystan
Street, London SW3 3NT
T: +44 (0)20 7590 9860
www.paintlibrary.co.uk

SPECIALIST FINISHES

MALCOLM CONNELL
+44 (0)1451 844680
www.specialistpainter.co.uk

P & C CZAINSKI
+44 (0)7771 624548
www.czainski.com

THE FINISHED EFFECT
+44 (0)7968 024104
www.thefinishedeffect.co.uk

LIZZIE PORTER
+44 (0)7956 551149
Email: lizziporter@aol.com

BRIAN WOOD
+44 (0)20 8539 2063
Email: bn.wood@hotmail.com

FABRICS

The Nicky Haslam fabric collection, 'Random Harvest', is available from Turnell & Gigon in the UK, Claremont in the USA and Primavera in Canada.

ABBOT AND BOYD
1/22 First Floor, North
Extension, Chelsea Harbour,
London SW10 0XE
+44 (0)20 7351 9985
www.abbottandboyd.co.uk

CLAREMONT
35 Elystan Street,
London SW3 3NT
+44 (0)20 7581 9575
1059 3rd Avenue, 2nd Floor,
New York, NY 10021, USA
+1 (0)212 486 1252
723 North La Cienga
Boulevard, Los Angeles, CA
90069, USA
+1 (0)310 248 3841
www.claremontfurnishing.com

THOMAS LAVIN
Pacific Design Center, 8687
Melrose Avenue, Suite B310, West
Hollywood, CA 90069, USA
+1 (0)310 278 2456
www.thomaslavin.com

PRIMAVERA
160 Pears Avenue, Suite 110,
Toronto, ON M5R 3P8, Canada
+1 (0)416 921 3334
www.primavera.ca

GEORGE SPENCER DESIGNS
33 Elystan Street,
London SW3 3NT
+44 (0)20 7584 3003
www.georgespencer.com

BERNARD THORPE
53 Chelsea Manor Street,
London SW3 5RZ
+44 (0)20 7352 5745
www.bernardthorp.co.uk

TURNELL & GIGON
410 The Chambers,
London SW10 0XF
+44 (0)20 7259 7280
www.turnellandgigongroup.com

CURTAINS

MAGENTA INTERIORS
Battersea Business Centre,
99–109 Lavender Hill,
London SW11 5QL
+44 (0)20 8571 1052
www.magentainteriors.co.uk

S C SADLER LTD
10A Thornsett Road,
London SW18 4EN
+44 (0)20 8874 1592
www.scsadler.co.uk

THOMSON-SHULTZ
Unit 6H, Beaver Industrial
Park, Chancerygate Southall,
Brent Road, Southall UB2 5FB
+44 (0)20 8571 1057
www.thomson-schultz.co.uk

PASSEMENTERIE

CASTILLA RIENDA SL
C/ Jaime I 27, P I
Mediterraneo, E46560,
Massalfassar, Valencia, Spain
+34 (0)961 417 044
www.castillarienda.com

SMITH & BRIGHTY
184 Walton Street, London
SW3 2JL
+44 (0)20 7823 8505

LINEN

GAYLE WARWICK
www.gaylewarwick.com
Available at Thomas Goode,
19 South Audley Street,
London W1K 2BN
+44 (0)20 7499 2823
www.thomasgoode.com

CARPETS

AM COLLECTIONS
584 Broadway, Suite 201,
New York, NY 10012, USA
+1 (0)212 625 2616
www.amcollections.com

BARTHOLOMEUS BVBA
Nieuwstraat 58, 8820 Torhout,
Belgium
+32 (0)50 21 22 27

BORDERLINE
Unit 1, Mercy Terrace,
Ladywell, London SE13 7UX
+44 (0)20 8690 4888
www.borderlinecps.com

CODIMAT COLLECTION
63–65, rue du Cherche-Midi,
75006 Paris, France
+33 (0)1 45 44 68 20
www.codimatcollection.com

LUKE IRWIN
22 Pimlico Road,
London SW1W 8LJ
+44 (0)20 7730 6070
www.lukeirwin.com

STARK CARPETS
Chelsea Harbour Design
Centre, London SW10 0XE
+44 (0)207 352 6001
www.starkcarpet.co.uk

TAI PING CARPETS
Chelsea Harbour,
406–407 Design Centre East,
London SW10 OXE
+44 (0)20 7808 9650
www.taipingcarpets.com

HARDWOOD

WHITE AND WHITE
White & White London, The
Barn, Coptfold Hall, Writtle
Road, Margaretting CM4 0EL
+44 (0)1277 353499
www.whiteandwhitelondon.com

STONE

BRITANNICUS STONE
Unit 24 Chelsea Wharf,
15 Lots Road,
London SW10 0QJ
+44 (0)20 7371 7299
www.britannicus-stone.co.uk

IDEAS2REALITY
PO Box 14, Knebworth,
Hertfordshire SG3 6RT
+44 (0)1438 811 186
www.ideas-2-reality.com

STONE INTERIORS
90 Old Woolwich Road,
London SE10 9PN
+44 (0)20 8293 9253
www.stoneinteriors.co.uk

STONE PRODUCTIONS
7–9 East Hill,
London SW18 2HT
+44 (0)20 8871 9257
www.stoneproductions.co.uk

HARDWARE

RÉMY GARNIER
30 bis, boulevard de la Bastille,
75012 Paris, France
+33 (0)1 43 43 84 85
www.garnier-remy.com

P E GEURIN
23 Jane Street,
New York, NY 10014, USA
+1 (0)212 243 5270
www.peguerin.com

MCKINNON & HARRIS
220 North Dome,
Design Centre Chelsea
Harbour, London SW10 0XE
+44 (0)20 7349 9685
211 East 59th Street,
New York, NY 10022, USA
+1 (0)212 371 8260
www.mckinnonharris.com

NANZ
20 Vandam Street,
New York, NY 10013, USA
+1 (0)212 367 7000
www.nanz.com

CS SCHMIDT
15–17 Passage de la Main d'Or,
75011 Paris, France
+33 (0)1 48 06 57 19
www.charles-schmidt.fr

CUSTOM-MADE FURNITURE

ARCHER AND SMITH
The Manor House, Chiseldon,
Swindon, Wiltshire SN4 0LN
+44 (0)1793 740375
www.archersmith.co.uk

RUPERT BEVAN (AND
SPECIALIST FINISHES)
40–44 Fulham High Street,
London SW6 3LQ
+44 (0)20 7731 1919
www.rupertbevan.com

BROWN JORDAN
(OUTDOOR FURNITURE)
9860 Gidley Street,
El Monte, CA 91731, USA
+1 800 743 4252 option 6
www.brownjordan.com

CHELSEA UPHOLSTERY
& INTERIORS
216 New King's Road,
London SW6 4NZ
+44 (0)207 384 1666
www.chelseaupholstery.co.uk

DUDGEON
1A Brompton Place,
London SW3 1QE
+44 (0)20 7589 0322
www.dudgeonsofas.com

LAM UPHOLSTERY
Blackbird Lane, Aldenham,
Watford WD25 8BS
+44 (0)1923 857 840
www.lamupholstery.com

LAWRENCE MERCER
+44 (0)7851 815 997
lawrencemercer@ntlworld.com

THOMAS MESSEL
Bradley Court,
Wotton-Under-Edge,
Gloucestershire GL12 7PP
+44 (0)1453 843 220
www.thomasmessel.com

OKA (including the
Nicky Haslam collection)
155–167 Fulham Road,
London SW3 6SN
(and shops nationwide)
+44 (0)20 7581 2574
+44 (0)844 815 7380
www.okadirect.com

BEN WHISTLER
9 Silver Road,
London W12 7SG
+44 (0)20 8576 6600
www.benwhistler.com

ANTIQUES

1 HUNDRED
Wisborough Green,
West Sussex (by appointment)
+44 (0)778 233 9699
www.1hundred.co

ANTIQUAIRES DE LIGNANE
Puymicard, 6110 Route
D'Avignon, Lignane 13540
Puyricard, France
Tel: +33 (0)4 42 92 38 28
www.antiquaire-lignane.com

ANDREW BEWICK
287 Lillie Road,
London SW6 7LL
+44 (0)20 7385 9025
www.lillieroad.co.uk

TARQUIN BILGEN
227 Ebury Street,
London, SW1W 8UT
+44 (0)207 259 0111
www.tarquinbilgen.com

JOHN BIRD ANTIQUES
The Clubroom, High Street,
Petworth, West Sussex
GU28 0AU
+44 (0)1798 343250
www.johnbirdantiques.com

BLOCH ANTIQUES
22 Church Street,
London NW8 8EP
+44 (0)20 7723 6575
www.angellantiques.com

BROWNRIGG DECORATIVE
ANTIQUES
511 King's Road,
London SW10 0TX
+44 (0)20 7353 7223
www.brownrigg-interiors.co.uk

CHRISTOPHER BUTTERWORTH
71 Pimlico Road,
London SW1W 8NE
+44 (0)20 7823 4554
www.christopherbutterworth.com

JF CHEN
941 North Highland Avenue,
Los Angeles, CA 90038, USA
+1 (0)310 559 2436
www.jfchen.com

CORE ONE
The Gasworks,
2 Michael Road,
London SW6 2AD
+44 (0)20 7731 7171
www.coreoneantiques.com

DEAN ANTIQUES LTD
Core One, The Gasworks
2 Michael Road, London
SW6 2AN
+44 (0)20 7610 6997
www.dean@deanantiques.com

DECORATIVE COLLECTIVE
Unit 8E, Millers Close,
Fakenham Industrial Estate,
Norfolk NR21 8NW
+44 (0)1328 856333
+44 (0)778 233 9699
www.decorativecollective.com

ORLANDO HARRIS – BLANCHARD
The Gas Works, 2 Michael
Row, London SW6 2AN
+44 (0)7836 729 487
www.jwblanchard.com

NICHOLAS HASLAM
12–14 Holbein Place,
London SW1 8NL
+44 (0)20 7730 8623
www.nicholashaslam.com

CHRISTOPHER HODSOLL
23 Berkley Square, London
W1J 6HE (by appointment)
+44 (0)20 7843 386 286
www.hodsoll.com

L'ISLE SUR LA SORGUE
(BIANNUAL ANTIQUES FAIR)
Avignon, France
+33 (0)4 90 38 04 78

JAMES JACKSON
279 Lillie Road,
London SW6 7LL
+44 (0)20 7385 9050

PATRICK JEFFERSON
69 Pimlico Road,
London SW1W 8NE
+44 (0)20 7730 6161
www.patrickjefferson.com

CHRISTOPHER JONES ANTIQUES
Pomfret House,
Easton Nesten, Towcester,
Northamptonshire
NN12 7HS
+44 (0)7775 900 436
www.christopherjonesantiques.co.uk

LASSCO SALVAGE
Brunswick House,
30 Wandsworth Road,
London SW8 2LG
+44 (0)20 7394 2100
or London Road, Milton
Common, Oxon OX9 2JN
+44 (0)1844 277188
www.lassco.co.uk

LIZ'S ANTIQUE HARDWARE
453 South La Brea Avenue,
Los Angeles, CA 90036, USA
+1 (0)323 939 4403
www.lahardware.com

LUDLOW RACECOURSE
ANTIQUES FAIR
Ludlow Racecourse,
Bromfield, Ludlow,
Shropshire SY8 2BT
+44 (0)1544 267481

MARCHAND ANTIQUES
40 Church Street,
London NW8 8EP
+44 (0)20 7724 9238
www.marchandantiques.co.uk

LIZ O'BRIEN
306 East 61st Street,
New York, NY 10065, USA
+1 (0)212 755 3800
www.lizobrien.com

PETWORTH ANTIQUES CENTRE
East Street, Petworth,
West Sussex GU28 0AB
+44 (0)1798 343178
www.petworthantiquecentre.co.uk

JOSEPHINE RYAN ANTIQUES
17 Langton Street,
London SW10 0JL
+44 (0)20 7352 5618
www.josephineryanantiques.co.uk

JOHN SALIBELLO
211 and 229 East 60th Street,
New York, NY 10022, USA
+1 (0)212 838 5767
www.johnsalibello.com

RICHARD SHAPIRO
8905 Melrose Avenue ,
Los Angeles, CA 09969, USA
+1 (0)310 275 6700
www.studiolo.com

SPENCER SWAFFER ANTIQUES
30 High Street, Arundel,
West Sussex BN18 9AB
+44 (0)1903 882132
www.spencerswaffer.co.uk

TALISMAN
79–91 New King's Road,
London SW6 4SQ
+44 (0)20 7731 4686
www.talismanlondon.com

ALEXANDER VON WESTENHOLZ
297 Lillie Road,
London SW6 7LL
+44 (0)20 7386 1888
www.avwantiques.com

JAMES WORRELL
2 Church Street,
London NW8 8ED
+44 (0)20 7563 7181
www.jamesworrall.com

LAMPS AND GLASSWARE

HECTOR FINCH
90 Wandsworth Bridge Road,
London, SW6 2TF
+44 (0)20 7731 8886
www.hectorfinch.com

THE LOUVRE MUSEUM SHOP
4 Place du Louvre,
75001, Paris, France
+33 (0)1 40 20 53 17
www.louvrefr/en

PHILIPS & WOOD
4 Wilson Walk, Prebend
Gardens, London W4 1TP
+44 (0)20 8222 8117
www.philipsandwood.co.uk

VAUGHAN LTD
G1, Chelsea Harbour Design
Centre, London SW10 0XE
+44 (0)20 7349 4600
www.vaughandesigns.com

VALERIE WADE
108 Fulham Road,
London SW3 6HS
+44 (0)20 7225 1414
www.valeriewade.com

WILLIAM YEOWARD
270 King's Road,
London SW3 5AW
+44 (0)20 7349 7828
www.williamyeoward.com

ART

ART
+44 (0)20 8435 6556
www.art.co.uk

HUGO DE FERRANTI
Hazlitt Holland-Hibbert,
38 Bury Street,
London SW1Y 6BB
+44 (0)20 7839 7600

CARINA HASLAM ART
91 High Street, Great
Missenden, Buckinghamshire
HP1 60A
+44 (0)1494 866914
www.carinahaslamart.com

SOPHIA KOOPMAN
21 Ellis Street,
London SW1X 9AL
+44 (0)203 0867 512
www.koopmancontemporaryart.com

BOB LAWRENCE GALLERY
84 Pimlico Road,
London SW1W 8LL
+44 (0)20 7730 5900

NEW ART CENTRE
Roche Court, East Winterslow,
Salisbury, Wiltshire SP5 1BG
+44 (0)1980 862244
www.sculpture.uk.com

THE PAINTBRUSH FACTORY
GroundFloor Group, Str.
Henri Barbusse nr. 59–6 Cluj-
Napoca, 400616 Romania
www.groundfloor.ro

PRINTS

ROGER SMITH PRINTS & FRAMING
London
+44 (0)7931 923688

RAMSAY PRINTS
227 Ebury Street,
London SW1W 8UT
+44 (0)20 7730 6776

FLORISTS

BURSTING BUDS
8 Clarendon Road, Holland
Park, London W11 3AA
+44 (0)20 7229 6930
www.burstingbuds.com

LONGACRES NURSERY
London Road, Bagshot,
Surrey GU19 5JB
+44 (0)1276 476778

PULLBROOK AND GOULD
Liscartan House, 127 Sloane
Street, London SW1X 9AS
+44 (0)20 7730 0030
www.pulbrookandgould.co.uk

BOOKSHOPS

HEYWOOD HILL
10 Curzon Street,
London W1J 5HH
+44 (0)20 7629 0647
www.heywoodhill.com

POTTERTON BOOKS
93 Lower Sloane Street,
London SW1W 8DA
+44 (0)20 7730 4235
www.pottertonbooks.co.uk

JOHN SANDOE
10 Blacklands Terrace,
London SW3 2SR
+44 (0)20 7589 9473
www.johnsandoe.com

FOOD AND DRINK

CLARKE'S
122 & 124 Kensington Church
Street, London, W8 4BH
+44 (0)20 7221 9225
www.sallyclarke.com

COATES AND SEELY
Woodlings Vineyard,
Harroway, Whitchurch,
Hampshire RG28 7QT
+44 (0)1256 892220
www.coatesandseely.com

NEWLYNS FARM SHOP
Lodge Farm, North
Warnborough, Hook,
Hampshire RG29 1HA
+44 (0)1256 704128
www.newlyns-farmshop.co.uk

SACRED SPIRITS CO
5 Talbot Road,
London N6 4QS
+44 (0)20 8340 0992
www.sacredspiritscompany.com

INDEX

Figures in *italics* refer to captions.

A

B

C

D

E

F

G

H

ACKNOWLEDGEMENTS

FLORA CONNELL, without whom the book would not have been possible.

RUTH BURGESS, who stepped into the breach whenever requested, and all my team at NH Design for their advice, patience and encouragement.

SUSAN CREWE, for writing so elegant a foreword.

MIN HOGG, for a lifetime of friendship and inspiration.

JOHN AND JEAN MAJOR, for their constant steadfastness of care of both myself and the Hunting Lodge.

MARTIN GOSLING and GERALD WEST, for their incomparable skill in maintaining the garden.

NASH CHOWDHURY, for his tireless dexterity in driving.

SIMON UPTON, for his superb photographs and unfailing good humour.

Archivist SHEILA MILLARD, for sharing her infinite erudition of the history of Hampshire in general and of Odiham and the Hunting Lodge in particular.

JACQUI SMALL, my publisher, and her associate publisher JO COPESTICK, for their faith in this book and for the sumptuously produced result. To all in their organization for their professional ability – and for turning a blind eye to many missed deadlines – specifically art director PAUL TILBY, for his immaculate design, project editor ZIA MATTOCKS, for editing the project with such enthusiasm, and managing editor LYDIA HALLIDAY, for her swift co-ordination.

Lastly, and most importantly, to the staff of THE NATIONAL TRUST at The Vyne, Hampshire – and especially SIR SIMON JENKINS – for their support and expertise, which make living at the Hunting Lodge so rewarding.

My profound gratitude to all of you.

Winter wonderland. Snow almost buries the Hunting Lodge in this photograph, taken by me in 2010.

Patricia Verperlen.

Valerie Van Langenhove

Maritzina Gore

Philip & Martin

Trevor

Gavin Houghton

Will Hutchinson

Louise Rainer

Adam Tyler-Moore

David Dawson

L. Freud Esqu.

Giles Hattersley

Hannah Rothschild

Mary Soames

Julian Berkeley

Michel & Christine

Susan Crewe.

Julian Berkeley

Sarah Mc Williams

Peter, Ann & Penny

Carole Bamford + Anthony

Caroline zu Ysenburg

Colette too!

Richard

David Jenkins

Clarissa

Victoria